John Macgregor

A Thousand Miles in the Rob Roy Canoe on Rivers and Lakes of Europe

John Macgregor

A Thousand Miles in the Rob Roy Canoe on Rivers and Lakes of Europe

ISBN/EAN: 9783337233518

Printed in Europe, USA, Canada, Australia, Japan

Cover: Foto ©Andreas Hilbeck / pixelio.de

More available books at **www.hansebooks.com**

A THOUSAND MILES

IN THE

ROB ROY CANOE

ON RIVERS AND LAKES OF EUROPE.

RAPIDS OF THE REUSS.　See page 150.

A

THOUSAND MILES

IN THE

ROB ROY CANOE

ON RIVERS AND LAKES OF

EUROPE.

BY J. MACGREGOR, M.A.,
TRINITY COLLEGE, CAMBRIDGE.

With Numerous Illustrations.

LONDON:
SAMPSON LOW, SON, AND MARSTON,
MILTON HOUSE, LUDGATE-HILL.
1866.

PREFACE.

The voyage about to be described was made last Autumn in a small Canoe, with a double paddle and sails, which the writer managed alone.

The route traversed by the Canoe led sometimes over mountains and through forests and plains, where the boat had to be carried or dragged.

The rivers, lakes, and canals navigated were as follows:—

The Rivers Thames, Sambre, Meuse, Rhine, Main, Danube, Reuss, Aar, Ill, Moselle, Meurthe, Marne, and Seine.

The Lakes Titisee, Constance, Unter See, Zurich, Zug, and Lucerne, together with six canals in Belgium and France, and two expeditions in the open sea of the British Channel.

TEMPLE, LONDON,
January, 1866.

LIST OF ILLUSTRATIONS.

	Page
RAPIDS OF THE REUSS (*Frontispiece*).	
SEA ROLLERS IN THE CHANNEL	19
SWIMMING HERD ON THE MEUSE	30
SINGERS' WAGGON ON THE DANUBE	51
A CROWD IN THE MORNING	67
HAYMAKERS AMAZED	84
NIGHT SURPRISE AT GEGGLINGEN	97
THE ROB ROY IN A CROWD	114
SAILING UPON LAKE ZUG	138
SHIRKING A WATERFALL	155
A CRITICAL MOMENT	171
ASTRIDE THE STERN	189
THE ROB ROY AND THE COW	215
POLITE TO THE LADIES	231
GROUP OF FRENCH FISHERS	247
PASSING A DANGEROUS BARRIER	264
A CHOKED CANAL	282
RIGGING ASHORE	291
CHART OF CURRENTS AND ROCKS	304

CONTENTS.

CHAPTER I.
GETTING READY.
Canoe Travelling— Other Modes—The Rob Roy—Hints—Tourists—The Rivers—The Dress—I and We—The Election 1

CHAPTER II.
THE START.
The Thames—The Channel—Ostend Canal—The Meuse—Holland—The Rhine—The Main—The Prince of Wales 12

CHAPTER III.
Hollenthal Pass—Black Forest—Beds—Lake Titisee—Storm—Source of the Danube 40

CHAPTER IV.
The Danube—Singers—Shady nooks—Geislingen—Morning Crowd—Islands—Monks—Concert—Fish—A race 57

CHAPTER V.
Sigmaringen—Treacherous trees—Congress of herons—Flying Dutchman—Tub and shovel—Bottle race—Snags—Ya Vol—Benighted 79

CHAPTER VI.
Day-dream—River Iller—Ulm—A stiff king—Lake Constance—Seeing in the dark—Coloured Canvas—Sign talk—Synagogue—Amelia 100

CHAPTER VII.
Fog—Fancy pictures—Boy soldiers—Boat's billet—Eating—Lake Zurich—Lake Zug—Swiss shots—Fishing Britons—Talk-book 122

CONTENTS.

CHAPTER VIII.

Sailing on Lucerne—Seeburg—River scenes—**Night** and snow—The Reuss—A dear dinner—Seeing a rope—Passing a fall—Bremgarten **rapids** 145

CHAPTER IX.

Music **at the** mill—Sentiment and chops—River Limmat—Fixed on a fall—On the river Aar—Falls of Lauffenburg—The cow **cart** 162

CHAPTER X.

Field of Foam—Precipice—Puzzled—Rheinfelden Rapids—Dazzled—Astride—Very Salt—The Ladies—Whirlpool—Funny **English**—**A** baby—The bride 180

CHAPTER XI.

Private concert—Thunderer—**La Hardt Forest—River Ill—**Madame Nico—Vosges—**Admirers—New wine** ... 199

CHAPTER XII.

Bonfire—My wife—Matthews—Tunnel picture—Imposture—Moselle—Cocher—Gymnastics—The paddle—A spell—Overhead—Feminine forum 217

CHAPTER XIII.

Epinal—The Tramp—Halcyon—Painted woman—Beating to quarters—Boat in a hedge—The Meurthe—Moving House—Tears **of a mother—Five francs** 235

CHAPTER XIV.

Ladies in muslin—Officers shouting—Volunteers' umbrella—Reims—**Leaks—Wet—**Madame Clicquot—Heavy blow—Dinner **talk—The** Elephant—Cloud 256

CHAPTER XV.

Hammering—Popish forms—Wise dogs—Blocked up—No **water**—Odd fellows—Dream on the Seine—Charing-**cross** 277

APPENDIX.

Hints **for** Canoists, with **a** Chart of hard rocks and difficult currents.

THE AUTHOR'S PROFITS WILL BE GIVEN TO THE ROYAL NATIONAL LIFE-BOAT INSTITUTION AND TO THE SHIPWRECKED MARINERS' SOCIETY.

CHAPTER I.

GETTING READY.

THE object of this book is to describe a new mode of travelling on the Continent, by which new people and things are met with, while healthy exercise is enjoyed, and an interest ever varied with excitement keeps fully alert the energies of the mind.

Some years ago the Water Lily was rowed by four men on the Rhine and on the Danube, and its "log" delighted all readers. Afterwards, the boat Water Witch laboured up French rivers, and through a hundred tedious locks on the Bâle canal. But these and other voyages of three or five men in an open boat were necessarily very limited. In the wildest parts of the best rivers the channel is too narrow for oars, or, if wide, it is too shallow for a row-boat; and the tortuous passages, the rocks and banks, the weeds and snags, the milldams, barriers, fallen trees, rapids, whirlpools, and waterfalls which constantly occur on a river winding among hills, make those very parts where the scenery is wildest and best to be quite unapproachable in an open boat, for it would be swamped by the sharp waves, or upset over the sunken rocks which are utterly impossible for a steersman to see.

But these very things, which are obstacles or dangers to the "pair oar," become interesting features to the voyager in a covered canoe. For now he looks forward, and not backward, as he sits in his little bark. He sees all his course, and the scenery besides. With one powerful sweep of his paddle he can instantly turn the canoe, when only a foot distant from fatal destruction. He can steer within an inch in a narrow place, or press through reeds and weeds, branches and grass; can hoist and lower his sail without changing his seat; can shove with his paddle when aground, or jump out in good time to prevent a decided smash. He can wade and haul the light craft over shallows, or on dry ground, through fields and hedges, over dykes, barriers, and walls; can carry it by hand up ladders and stairs, and can transport his boat over high mountains and broad plains in a cart drawn by a horse, a bullock, or a cow.

Nay, more than this, the covered canoe is

far stronger than an open boat, and may be fearlessly dropped headforemost into a deep pool, or a lock, or a millrace, and yet, when the breakers are high, in the open sea or fresh water rapids, they can only wash over the covered deck, while it is always dry within.

Again, the canoe is safer than a rowing-boat, because you sit so low in it, and never require to shift your place or lose hold of the paddle; while for comfort during long hours, for days and weeks of hard work, it is evidently the best, because you lean all the time against a backboard, and the moment you rest the paddle on your lap you are as much at ease as in an arm-chair; so that, while drifting along with the current or the wind, you can gaze around, and eat or read or chat with the starers on the bank, and yet, in a moment of sudden danger, the hands are at once on the faithful paddle ready for action.

Finally, you can lie at full length in the canoe, with the sail as an awning for the sun, or a shelter for rain, and you can sleep in it thus at night, under cover, with an opening for air to leeward, and at least as much room for turning in your bed as sufficed for the great Duke of Wellington; or, if you are tired of the water for a time, you can leave your boat at an inn—it will not be "eating its head off," like a horse; or you can send it home or sell it, and take to the road yourself, or sink into the dull old cushions of the "Première Classe," and dream you are seeing the world.

With such advantages, then, and with good weather and good health, the canoe voyage about to be described was truly delightful, and I never enjoyed so much continuous pleasure in any other tour.

But, before this deliberate assertion has weight with intending "canoeists," it may well be asked, from one who thus praises the paddle, "Has he travelled in other ways, so as to know their several pleasures? Has he climbed glaciers and volcanoes, dived into caves and catacombs, trotted in the Norway carriole, and galloped on the Russian steppes? Does he know the charms of a Nile boat, or a sail in the Ægean, or a mule in Spain; or has he ever swung on a camel, or glided on a sleigh, or trundled along in a Rantoone?"

Yes, he has most thoroughly enjoyed these and other modes of locomotion in the four quarters of the world; but the pleasure in the canoe was far better than all.

The weather this summer was, indeed, exceptionally good; but then rain would have diminished some of the difficulties, though it might have been a bore to paddle ten hours in a downpour. Two inches more of water in the rivers would have saved many a grounding, and the wading in consequence, and, at worst, the rain could have wetted only the upper man, which a cape can **cover;** so, even in bad weather, **give** me the canoe.

Messrs. Searle and Sons, of Lambeth, soon built for me the very boat I wanted.

The Rob Roy is built of oak, and covered fore and aft with cedar. She is made just short enough to go into the German railway waggons; that is to say, fifteen feet in length, twenty-eight inches broad, nine inches deep, weighs eighty pounds, and draws three inches of water, with an inch keel. A paddle seven feet long, with a blade at each end, **and a lug** sail and jib, are the means of propulsion; and a pretty blue silk Union Jack is the only ornament.

The elliptic hole in which I sit is fifty-four inches long and twenty broad, and has a mackintosh **cover** fastened round the combing and to a **button on** my breast; while between my knees **is** my baggage for three months, in a black bag one foot square and five inches deep.

But, having got this little boat, the difficulty was to **find** where she could **go to,** or what rivers were at once feasible **to paddle on,** and pretty **to** see.

Inquiries in London as to this had no result. Even the Paris Boat Club knew nothing of French rivers. The best German and Austrian maps were frequently wrong. They made villages on the banks which I found were a mile away in a wood, and so were useless to one who had made up his mind (a good resolve) never to leave his boat.

It was soon, therefore, evident that, after quitting the Rhine, this was to be a voyage of discovery. And as I would most gladly have accepted any hints on the matter myself, so I venture to hope that this narrative will lessen the trouble, while it stimulates the desire of the numerous travellers who will spend their vacation in a canoe.*

Not that I shall attempt to make a "handbook" to any of the streams. The man who has a spark of enterprize would turn from a river of which every reach was mapped and its channels all lettered. Fancy the free traveller, equipped for a delicious summer of savage life, quietly submitting to be cramped and tutored by a "Chart of the Upper Mosel," in the style of the following extracts copied literally from two guide-books :—

* See Appendix. Special hints for those who intend to "canoe it" will usually be given in the footnotes, or in the Appendix.

(1) "Turn to the r. (right), cross the brook, and ascend by a broad and steep forest track (in 40 min.) to the hamlet of Albersbach, situate in the midst of verdant meadows. In five min. more a cross is reached, where the path to the l. must be taken; in 10 min. to the r., in the hollow, to the saw mill; in 10 min. more through the gate to the r.; in 3 min. the least trodden path to the l. leading to the Gaschpels Hof; after ¼ hr. the stony track into the wood must be ascended," &c., &c.—*From B——'s Rhine, p.* 94.

(2) "*To the ridge of the Riffelberg* 8,000 ft. *Hotel* on top very good. 2 hrs. up. Guide 4 fr. Horse and man 10 fr. Path past the Church: then l. over fields: then up through a wood 1 hr. Past châlets: then r. across a stream."—*——'s Handbook*.

This sort of guide-book is not to be ridiculed. It is useful for some travellers as a ruled copy-book is of use to some writers. For first tours it may be needful and pleasant to have all made easy, to be carried in steamers or railways like a parcel, to stop at hotels Anglified by the crowd of English guests, and to ride, walk, or drive among people who know already just what you will want to eat, and see, and do.

Year after year it is enough of excitement to some tourists to be shifted in squads from town to town, according to the routine of an excursion ticket. Those who are a little more advanced will venture to devise a tour from the mazy pages of Bradshaw, and with portmanteau and bag, and hat-box and sticks, they find more than enough of judgment and tact is needed when they arrive in a night train, and must fix on an omnibus in a strange town. Safe at last in the bedroom of the hotel, they cannot but exclaim with relief and satisfaction "Well, here we are all right at last."

But after mountains and caves, churches and galleries, ruins and battle-fields have been pretty well seen, and after tact and fortitude have been educated by experience, the tourist is ready for new lines of travel which might have given him at first more anxiety than pleasure, and these he will find in deeper searches among the natural scenery and national character of the very countries he has only skimmed before.

The rivers and streams on the Continent are scarcely known to the English tourist, and the beauty and life upon them no one has well seen.

In his guide-book route, indeed, from town to town, the tourist has crossed this and that stream—has admired a few yards of the water, and has then left it for ever. He is carried again on a noble

THE DRESS.

river by night in a steamboat, or is whisked along its banks in a railway, and, between two tunnels, gets a moment's glimpse at the lovely water, and lo! it is gone.

But a mine of rich beauty remains there to be explored, and fresh gems of life and character are waiting to be gathered. These are not mapped and labelled and ticketed in any handbook yet; and far better so, for the enjoyment of such treasures is enhanced to the best traveller by the energy and pluck required to get at them.

On this new world of waters we are to launch the boat, the man, and his baggage, for we must describe all three,

"Arma virumque canoe."

So what sort of dress did he wear?

The clothes I took for this tour consisted of a complete suit of grey flannel for use in the boat, and another suit of light but ordinary dress for shore work and Sundays.

The "Norfolk jacket" is a loose frock-coat, like a blouse, with shoulder-straps, and belted at the waist, and garnished by six pockets. With this excellent new-fashioned coat, a something in each of its pockets, and a Cambridge straw hat, canvas wading shoes, blue spectacles, a waterproof overcoat, and my spare jib for a sun shawl, there was sure to be a full day's enjoyment in defiance of rain or sun, deeps or shallows, hunger or *ennui*.

Four hours' work to begin, and then three of rest or floating, reading or sailing, and again, a three hours' heavy pull, and then with a swim in the river or a bath at the inn, a change of garments and a pleasant walk, all was made quite fresh again for a lively evening, a hearty dinner, talk, books, pictures, letters, and bed.

Now I foresee that in the description of this tour I shall have to write "I," and the word "me" must be used by me very often indeed; but having the misfortune to be neither an Emperor, an editor, nor a married man, who can speak in the plural, I cannot help it if I am put down as a bachelor *egotist*, reserving the "we" for myself and my boat.

The manner of working the double-bladed paddle was easily learned by a few days' practice on the Thames, and so excellent is the exercise for the muscles of the limbs and body that I have continued it at intervals, even during the winter, when a pretty sharp "look out" must be kept to pilot safely among the red and yellow lights of steamers, barges, embankments, and bridges in an evening's voyage from Putney to Westminster.

All being ready and the weather very hot at the end of July, when the country had caught the election fever, and M.P.'s had run off to scramble for seats, and the lawyers had run after them to thicken the bustle, and the last bullet at Wimbledon had come "thud" on the target, it was time for the Rob Roy to start.

CHAPTER II.

THE START.

The Thames—The Channel—Ostend Canal—The Meuse—Holland—The Rhine—The Main—The Prince of Wales.

The Rob Roy bounded away joyously on the top of the tide through Westminster Bridge, and swiftly shooting the narrow piles at Blackfriars, danced along the waves of the Pool, which looked all golden in the morning sun, but were in fact of veritable pea-soup hue.

A fine breeze at Greenwich enabled me to set the new white sail, and we skimmed along with a cheery hissing sound. At such times the river is a lively scene with steamers and sea-bound ships, bluff little tugs, and big looming barges. I had many a chat with the passing sailors, for it was well to begin this at once, seeing that every day afterwards I was to have talk with the river folk in English, French, Dutch, German, or else some hotchpot patois.

The bargee is not a bad fellow if you begin with good humour, but he will not stand banter. Often they began the colloquy with, "Any room for another?" or, "Got your life insured, governor?" but I smiled and nodded to every one, and every one on every river and lake was friendly to me.

Gravesend was to be the port for the night, but Purfleet looked so pretty that I took a tack or two to reconnoitre, and resolved to stop at the very nice hotel on the river, which I beg to recommend.

While lolling about in my boat at anchor in the hot sun a fly stung my hand; and although I did not remark it at once, the arm speedily swelled, and I had to poultice the hand at night and to go to church next day with a sling, which appendage excited a great deal of comment in the village Sunday-school. This little incident is mentioned because it was the only occasion on which any insect troubled me on the voyage, though several croakers had predicted that in rivers and marshes there would be hundreds of wasps, venomous flies, and gnats, not to mention other residents within doors.

Just as I entered the door of the quiet little church, an old gentleman about to go in fell down dead on the path. It was impossible not to be much impressed with this sudden death as a solemn warning, especially to one in vigorous health.

The "Cornwall" Reformatory School-ship is moored at Purfleet. Some of the boys came ashore for a walk, neatly clad and very well behaved. Captain Burton, who commands this interesting vessel, received me on board very kindly, and the evening service between decks was a sight to remember for ever.

About 100 boys sat in rows along the old frigate's main-deck, with the open ports looking on the river, now reddened by a setting sun, and the cool air pleasantly fanning us. The lads chanted the Psalms to the music of a harmonium, played with excellent feeling and good taste, and the Captain read a suitable portion from some selected book, and then prayer was offered; and all this was by and for poor vagrant boys, whose claim on society is great indeed if measured by the wrong it has done them in neglect if not in precept, nay, even in example.

Next morning the canoe was lowered down a ladder from the hay-loft, where it had been kept (it had to go up into many far more strange places in subsequent days), and the Cornwall boys bid me a pleasant voyage—a wish most fully realized indeed.

After taking in supplies at Gravesend, I shoved off into the tide, and lit a cigar, and now I felt I had fairly started. Then there began a strange feeling of *freedom* and *novelty* which lasted to the end of the tour.

Something like it is felt when you first march off with a knapsack ready to walk anywhere, or start alone in a sailing-boat for a long cruise.

But then in walking you are bounded by every sea and river, and in a common sailing-boat you are bounded by every shallow and shore; whereas, I was in a canoe, which could be paddled or sailed, hauled, or carried over land or water to Rome, if I liked, or to Hong-Kong.

The wind was fair again, and up went my sail. The reaches got wider and the water more salt, but I knew every part of the course, for I had once spent a fortnight about the mouth of the Thames in my pretty little sailing-boat, the Kent, alone, with only a dog, a chart, a compass, and a bachelor's kettle.

The new steamer Alexandra, which plies from London daily, passed me here, with its high-terraced American decks covered with people, and the crowd gave a fine loud cheer to the Rob Roy, for the newspapers had mentioned its departure. Presently the land seemed to fade away at each side in pale distance, the water got salt, and it was more sea than river, till near the Nore we entered a great shoal of porpoises. Often as I have seen these harmless and agile playfellows I had never been so close before, and in a boat so small as to be almost disregarded by them, wily though they be. I allowed the canoe to rock on the waves, and the porpoises frequently came near enough to be struck by my paddle, but I did not wage war, for a flap of a tail would have soon turned me upside down.

After a pleasant sail to Southend and along the beach, the wind changed, and a storm of heavy rain had to be met in its teeth by taking to the paddle, until I reached Shoeburyness, where I meant to stop a day or two in the camp of the National Artillery Association, which was assembled here for its first prize shooting.

The Royal Artillery received us volunteers on this occasion with the greatest kindness, and as they had appropriated quarters of officers absent on leave for the use of members of the Council of the Association, I was soon comfortably ensconced. The camp, however, in a wet field was moist enough; but the fine tall fellows who had come from Yorkshire, Somerset, or Aberdeen to handle the 68-pounders, trudged about in the mud with good humour and thick boots, and sang round the camp-fire in a drizzle of rain, and then pounded away at the targets next day, for these were volunteers of the right sort.

As the wind had then risen to a gale it seemed a good opportunity for a thorough trial of the canoe in rough water, and I paddled her to a corner where she would be least injured by being thrown ashore after an upset, and where I could leave her safe while I might run to change clothes after a swim.

The buoyancy of the boat astonished me, and her stability was in every way satisfactory. In the midst of the waves I even managed to rig up the mast and sail, and as I had no baggage on board and so did not mind being perfectly wet through in the experiments, there was nothing left untried, and the confidence then gained for after times was invaluable.

Early next morning I started directly in the teeth of the wind, and paddled against a very heavy sea to Southend, where I got a nice warm bath while my clothes were getting dried, and then the Rob Roy had its first railway journey in one of the little cars on the Southend pier.

It was amusing to see how much interest and curiosity the canoe excited even on the Thames, where all kinds of new and old and wonderful boats may be seen. The reasons for this I never exactly made out. Some wondered to see so small a boat at sea, others had never seen a canoe before, the manner of rowing was new to most, and the sail made many smile. The graceful shape of the boat pleased others, the cedar covering and the jaunty flag, and a good many stared at the captain's uniform, and they stared more after they had asked, "Where are you going to?" and were told, "I really do not know."

From Sheerness to Dover was the route, and to begin with, on the branch line train the Rob Roy had to be carried on the coals in the engine-tender, with torrents of rain and plenty of hot sparks driven into her by the gale; but after some delay at a junction the canoe was formally introduced to a baggage-waggon and ticketed like a portmanteau, the first of a series of transits in this way.

The London Chatham and Dover Railway Company took this new kind of "box" as passengers' luggage, so I had nothing to pay, and the steamer to Ostend was equally large-hearted, so I say, "Canoemen, choose this channel."

But before crossing to Belgium I had a day at Dover, where I bought some stuff and had a jib made for the boat by deft and fair fingers, and paddled the Rob Roy on the green

SAILING ON THE SEA.

Rollers off the Digue.

waves which toss about off the pier-head most delectably. The same performance was repeated on the top of the swell, tumbling and breaking on the "digue"* at Ostend, where, even with little

* At Ostend I found an English gentleman preparing for a voyage on the Danube, for which he was to build a "centre board" boat. Although no doubt a sailing boat could reach the Danube by the Bamberg canal, yet, after four tours on that river from its source as far as Pest, I am convinced that to trust to sailing upon it would entail much tedious delay, useless trouble, and constant anxiety. If the wind is ahead you have all the labour of

wind, the rollers ran high on a strong ebb tide. Fat bathers wallowed in the shallows, and fair ones, dressed most bizarre, were swimming like ducks. All of these, and the babies squalling hysterically at each dip, were duly admired; and then I had a quieter run under sail on their wide and straight canal.

With just a little persuasion the railway people consented to put the canoe in the baggage-van, and to charge a franc or two for "extra luggage" to Brussels. Here she was carried on a cart through the town to another station, and in the evening we were at Namur, where the Rob Roy was housed for the night in the landlord's private parlour, resting gracefully upon two chairs.

Two porters carried her through the streets next morning, and I took a paddle on the Sambre, but very soon turned down stream and smoothly glided to the Meuse.

Glancing water, brilliant sun, a light boat, and a light heart, all your baggage on board, and on a

tacking, and are frequently in slack water near the banks, and often in channels where the only course would be dead to windward. If the wind is aft the danger of "running" is extreme where you have to "broach to" and stop suddenly near a shallow or a barrier. With a strong side wind, indeed, you can sail safely, but this must come from north or south, and the high banks vastly reduce its effect.

fast current,—who would exchange this for any diligence or railway, or steamboat, or horse? A pleasant stream was enough to satisfy at this early period of the voyage, for the excitement of rocks and rapids had not yet become a charm, nay, as it was afterwards, almost a necessity.

It is good policy, too, that a quiet, easy, respectable sort of river like the Meuse should be taken in the earlier stage of a water tour. The river-banks one would call tame if seen from shore are altogether new when you open up the vista from the middle of the stream. The picture that is rolled sideways to the common traveller now pours out from before you, ever enlarging from a centre, and in the gentle sway of the stream the landscape seems to swell on this side and that with new things ever advancing to meet you in succession.

How careful I was at the first shallow! getting out and wading as I lowered the boat. A month afterwards I would dash over them with a shove here and a stroke there in answer to a hoarse croak of the stones at the bottom grinding against my keel.

And the first barrier—how anxious it made me, to think by what means shall I get over. A man appeared just in time (N.B.—They *always* do), and twopence made him happy for his share of carrying the boat round by land, and I jumped in again as before.

Sailing was easy, too, in a fine wide river, strong and deep, and with a favouring breeze, and when the little steamer passed I drew alongside and got my penny roll and penny glass of beer, while the wondering passengers (the first of many amazed foreigners) smiled, chattered, and then looked grave—for was it not indecorous to laugh at an Englishman evidently mad, poor fellow?

The voyage was chequered by innumerable little events, all perfectly different from those one meets on shore, and when I came to the forts at Huy and knew the first day's work was closing, the persuasion was complete that quite a new order of sensations had been set going.

Next morning I found the boat safe in the coach-house and the sails still drying on the harness-pegs, where I had left them, but the ostler and all his folks were nowhere to be seen. Everybody had gone to join the long funeral procession of a great musician, who was celebrated at Huy and lived there fifty years.

The pleasure of meandering with a new river is very peculiar and fascinating. Each few yards brings a novelty, or starts an excitement. A crane jumps up here, a duck flutters there, splash leaps a gleaming trout by your side, the rushing sound of rocks warns you round that corner, or anon you come suddenly upon a millrace. All these, in addition to the scenery and the people and the weather, and the determination that you *must* get on, over, through, or under every difficulty, and cannot leave your boat in a desolate wold, and ought to arrive at a house before dark, and that your luncheon bag is long since empty; all these, I say, keep the mind awake, which would perchance dose away for 100 miles in a first-class carriage.

It is, as in the voyage of life, that our cares and hardships are our very Mentors of living. Our minds would only vegetate if all life were like a straight canal, and we in a boat being towed along it. The afflictions that agitate the soul are as its shallows, rocks, and whirlpools, and the bark that has not been tossed on billows knows not half the sweetness of the harbour of rest.

The river soon got fast and lively, and hour after hour of vigorous work prepared one well for breakfast. Trees seemed to spring up in front and grow tall, but it was only because I came rapidly towards them. Pleasant villages floated as it were to meet me, gently moving. All life got to be a smooth and gliding thing, without fuss and without dust or anything sudden or loud, till at length the bustle and hammers of Liege neared the Rob Roy—for it was always the objects and not myself that seemed to move. Here I saw a fast steamer, the Seraing, propelled by water forced from its sides, and as my boat hopped and bobbed in the steamer's waves we entered a dock together, and I hoisted the canoe into a garden for the night.

Gun-barrels are the rage in Liege. Everybody there makes or carries or sells gun-barrels. Even women walk about with twenty stocked rifles on their backs, and each rifle, remember, weighs 10 lbs. They sell plenty of fruit in the market, and there are churches well worth a visit here, but gun-barrels, after all, are the prevailing idea of the place.

However, it is not my purpose to describe the towns seen on this tour. I had seen Liege well, years before, and indeed almost every town mentioned in these pages. The charm then of the voyage was not in going to strange lands, but in seeing old places in a new way.

Here at length the Earl of Aberdeen met me. He had got a canoe built for the trip, but a foot longer and two inches narrower than the Rob Roy, and, moreover, made of fir instead of strong oak. It was sent from London to Liege, and the "combing" round the edge of the deck was broken in the journey, so we spent some hours at a cabinet-maker's, where it was neatly mended.

Launching our boats unobserved on the river, we soon left Liege in the distance and braved the hot sun.

The pleasant companionship of two travellers, each quite free in his own boat, was very enjoyable. Sometimes we sailed, then paddled a mile or two, or joined to help the boats over a weir, or towed them along while we walked on the bank for a change.*

Each of us took whichever side of the river pleased him best, and we talked across long acres of water between, to the evident surprise of sedate people on the banks, who often could see only one of the strange elocutionists, the other being hidden by bushes or tall sedge. When talking thus aloud had amplified into somewhat uproarious

---

* Frequent trials afterwards convinced me that towing is only useful if you feel very cramped from sitting. And this constraint is felt less and less as you get accustomed to sit ten or twelve hours at a time. Experience enables you to make the seat perfectly comfortable, and on the better rivers you have so frequently to get out that any additional change is quite needless. Towing is slower progress than paddling, even when your arms are tired, though I found the boat so light to tow that for miles I have drawn it by my little finger on a canal.

singing, the chorus was far more energetic than harmonious, but then the Briton is at once the most timid and shy of mortal travellers, and the most *outré* and singular when he chooses to be free.

The midday beams on a river in August are sure to conquer your fresh energies at last, and so we had to pull up at a village for bread and wine.

The moment I got into my boat again a shrill whining cry in the river attracted attention, and I saw it came from a poor little boy, who had somehow fallen into the water, and was now making his last faint efforts to cling to a great barge in the stream. Naturally I rushed over to save him, and my boat went so fast and so straight that its sharp prow caught the hapless urchin in the rear, and with such a pointed reminder that he screamed and struggled and thus got safely on the barge, which was beyond his reach, until thus roughly but fortunately aided.

On most of the Belgian, German, and French rivers there are excellent floating baths, an obvious convenience which I do not recollect observing on a single river in Britain, though in summer we have quite as many bathers as there are abroad.

The floating bath consists of a wooden framework, say 100 feet long, moored in the stream, and through which the water runs freely, while a set of strong bars and chains and iron network forms a false bottom, shallow at one end and deeper at the other, so that the bather cannot be carried away by the current.

Round the sides there are bathing boxes and steps, ladders, and spring boards for the various degrees of aquatic proficiency.

The youths and even the little boys on the Rhine are very good swimmers, and many of them dive well. Sometimes there is a ladies' bath of similar construction, from which a good deal of very lively noise may be heard when the fair bathers are in a talkative mood.

The soldiers at military stations near the rivers are marched down regularly to bathe, and one day we found a large number of young recruits assembled for their general dip.

While some were in the water others were firing at the target for ball practice. There were three targets, each made of cardboard sheets, fastened upon wooden uprights. A marker safely protected in a ball-proof *mantelet* was placed so close to these targets that he could see all three at once. One man of the firing party opposite each party having fired, his bullet passed through the pasteboard and left a clear round hole in it, while the ball itself was buried in the earth behind, and so could be recovered again, instead of being dashed into fragments as on our iron targets, and then spattered about on all sides, to the great danger of the marker and everybody else.

When three men had thus fired, signals were made by drum, flag, and bugle, and the firing ceased. The marker then came out and pointed to the bullet-mark on each target, and having patched up the holes he returned within his mantelet, and the firing was resumed. This very safe and simple method of ball practice is much better than that used in our military shooting.

Once as we rounded a point there was a large herd of cattle swimming across the stream in close column. I went right into the middle of them to observe how they would welcome a stranger. In the Nile you see the black oxen swim over the stream night and morning, reminding you of Pharaoh's dream about the "kine" coming out of the river, a notion that used to puzzle in boyhood days, but which is by no means an incongruous association of ideas when thus explained. The Bible is a book that bears full light to be cast upon it, for truth looks more true under more light.

We had been delayed this morning in our start,

CATTLE SWIMMING THE MEUSE.

and so the evening fell sombre ere we came near the resting-place. This was the town of Maastricht, in Holland, and it is stated to be one of the most strongly fortified places in Europe; that is, of course, of the old fashion, with straight high walls quite impervious to the Armstrong and Whitworth guns—of a century gone by.

But all we knew as we came near it at night was, that the stream was good and strong, and that no lights appeared. Emerging from trees we were right in the middle of the town, but where were the houses? had they no windows, no lamps, not even a candle?

Two great high walls bounded the river, but not a gate or port could we find, though one of us carefully scanned the right and the other cautiously scraped along the left of this very strange place.

It appears that the commerce and boats all turn into a canal above the old tumble-down fortress, and so the miserable blank brick sides bounded us thus inhospitably. Soon we came to a bridge, looming overhead in the blackness, and our arrival was greeted by a shower of stones from some Dutch lads upon it, pattering pitilessly upon the delicate cedar-covered canoes.

Turning up stream, and after a closer scrutiny, we found a place where we could cling to the wall, which here sloped a little with debris, and now there was nothing for it but to haul the boats up bodily over the impregnable fortification, and thus carry them into the sleepy town. No wonder the *octroi* guard stared as his lamp-light fell on two gaunt men in grey, carrying what seemed to him a pair of long coffins, but he was a sensible though surprised individual, and he guided us well, stamping through the dark deserted streets to an hotel.

Though the canoes in a cart made a decided impression at the railway-station next day, and arguments logically proved that the boats must go as baggage, the porters were dense to conviction, and obdurate to persuasion, until all at once they caught up the two neglected "batteaux," ran with them to the luggage-van, pushed them in, and banged the door, piped the whistle, and as the train went off—"Do you know why they have yielded so suddenly?" said a Dutchman, who could speak English. "Not at all," said we. "Because I told them one of you was the son of the Prime Minister, and the other Lord Russell's son."

But a change of railway had to be made at Aix-la-Chapelle, and after a hard struggle we had nearly surrendered the boats to the "merchandise train," to limp along the line at night and to arrive "perhaps to-morrow." Indeed the superintendent of that department seemed to clutch the boats as his prize, but as he gloried a little too loudly, the chief of the passengers' baggage came, listened, and with calm mien ordered for us a special covered truck, and on arriving at Cologne there was "nothing to pay."*

To be quiet we went to the Belle Vue, at Deutz, which is opposite Cologne, but a great singing society had its gala there, and sang and drank prodigiously. Next day (Sunday too) this same quiet Deutz had a "Schutzen Fest," where the

---

* This is an exceptional case, and I wrote from England to thank the officer. It would be unreasonable again to expect any baggage to be thus favoured. A canoe is at best a clumsy inconvenience in the luggage-van, and no one can wonder that it is objected to. In France the railway *fourgons* are shorter than in other countries, and the officials there insisted on treating my canoe as merchandise. The instances given above show what occurred in Belgium and Holland. In Germany little difficulty was made about the boat as luggage. In Switzerland there was no objection raised, for was I not an English traveller? As for the English railway guards, they have the good sense to see that a long light article like a canoe can be readily carried on the top of a passenger carriage. Probably some distinct rules will be instituted by the railways in each country, when they are found to be liable to a nautical incursion, but after all one can very well arrange to walk or see sights now and then, while the boat travels slower by a goods-train.

D

man who had hit the target best was dragged about in an open carriage with his wife, both wearing brass crowns, and bowing royally to a screaming crowd, while blue lights glared and rockets shot up in the serene darkness.

At Cologne, while Lord A. went to take our tickets at the steamer, the boats were put in a handcart, which I shoved from behind as a man pulled it in front. In our way to the river I was assailed by a poor vagrant sort of fellow, who insisted on being employed as a porter, and being enraged at a refusal he actually took up a large stone and ran after the cart in a threatening passion. I could not take my hands from the boats, though I feared his missile would smash them if he threw it, but I kicked up my legs behind as we trotted along. One of the sentries saw the man's conduct, and soon a policeman brought him to me as a prisoner, but as he trembled now with fear more than before with anger, I declined to make any charge, though the police pressed this course, saying, "Travellers are sacred here." This incident is mentioned because it was the sole occasion when any discourtesy happened to me during this tour.

We took the canoes by steamer to a wide part of the Rhine at Bingen. Here the scenery is good, and we spent an active day on the river, sailing in a splendid breeze, landing on islands, scudding about in steamers' waves, and, in fact, enjoying a combination of yacht voyage, pic-nic, and boat race.

This was a fine long day of pleasure, though in one of the sudden squalls my canoe happened to ground on a bank just at the most critical time, and the bamboo mast broke short. The uncouth and ridiculous appearance of a sail falling overboard is like that of an umbrella turned inside out in a gust of wind. But I got another stronger mast, and made the broken one into a boom.

Lord Aberdeen went by train to inspect the river Nahe, but reported unfavourably; and I paddled up from its mouth, but the water was very low.

Few arguments were needed to stop me from going against stream; for I have a profound respect for the universal principle of gravitation, and quite allow that in rowing it is well to have it with you by always going down stream, and so the good rule was to make steam, horse, or man take the canoe against the current, and to make gravity help the boat to carry me down.

Time pressed for my fellow-paddler to return quickly home, so we went on to Mayence, and thence by rail to Asschaffenburg. The canoes again travelled in grand state, having a truck to themselves; but instead of the stately philosopher superintendent of Aix-la-Chapelle, who managed this gratuitously, we had a fussy little person to deal with, and to pay accordingly,—the only case of decided cheating I can recollect during the voyage.

A fellow-passenger in the railway was deeply interested about our tour; and we had spoken of its various details for some time to him before we found that he supposed we were travelling with "two small cannons," mistaking the word "canôts" for "canons." He had even asked about their length and weight, and had heard with perfect placidity that our "canons" were fifteen feet long, and weighed eighty pounds, and that we took them only for "plaisir," not to sell. Had we carried two pet camelopards, he probably would not have been astonished.

The guests at the German inn of this long-named town amused us much by their respectful curiosity. Our dress in perfect unison, both alike in grey flannel, puzzled them exceedingly; but this sort of perplexity about costume and things in general was an everyday occurrence for weeks and months afterwards with me.

A fine breeze enabled us to start on the river Main under sail, though we lost much time in forcing the boats to do yachts' work; I am nclined to believe that sailing on rivers is rather a mistake unless with a favourable wind. The Main is an easy stream to follow, and the scenery only so-so. A storm of rain at length made it lunch-time, so we sheltered ourselves in a bleak sort of arbour attached to an inn, where they could give us only sour black bread and raw bacon. Eating this poor cheer in a wet, rustling breeze and pattering rain, half chilled in our mackintoshes, was the only bad fare I had, so little of "roughing it" was there in the after days of my luxurious tour.

With the afternoon came fine weather and pleasure again,—nay, positive sporting; for there were wild ducks quite impudent in their familiarity, and herons wading about with that look of injured innocence they put on when you dare to disturb them. So my friend capped his revolver-pistol, and I acted as a pointer dog, stealing along the other side of the river, and indicating the position of the game with my paddle.

Vast trouble was taken. Lord A. went ashore, and crawled on the bank a long way on his stomach to a wily bird, but, though the sportsman had shown himself at Wimbledon to be one of the best shots in the world, it was evidently not easy to shoot a heron with a pocket revolver.

As the darker shades fell, even this rather

stupid river became beautiful; and our evening bath was in a quiet pool, with pure yellow sand to rest on if you tired in swimming. At Hanau we stopped for the night.

The wanderings and turnings of the Main next day have really left no impression on my memory, except that we had a pleasant time, and at last came to a large Schloss, where we observed on the river a boat evidently English. While we examined this craft, a man told us it belonged to the Prince of Wales, "and he is looking at you now from the balcony."

For this was the Duchess of Cambridge's Schloss at Rumpenheim, and presently a four-in-hand crossed the ferry, and the Prince and Princess of Wales drove in it by the river-side, while we plied a vigorous paddle against the powerful west wind until we reached Frankfort, where our wet jackets were soon dried at the *Russie,* one of the best hotels in Europe.

The Frankfort boatmen were much interested next day to see the two English canoes flitting about so lightly on their river; sometimes skimming the surface with the wind, and despising the contrary stream; then wheeling about, and paddling hither and thither in shallows where it seemed as if the banks were only moist.

On one occasion we both got into my canoe,

and it supported the additional weight perfectly well, which seemed to prove that the dimensions of it were unnecessarily large for the displacement required. However, there was not room for both of us to use our paddles comfortably in the same canoe.

On the Sunday, the Royal personages came to the English church at Frankfort, and, with that quiet behaviour of good taste which wins more admiration than any pageantry, they walked from the place of worship like the rest of the hearers.

There is a true grandeur in simplicity when the occasion is one of solemn things.

Next day my active and pleasant companion had to leave me on his return to England. Not satisfied with a fortnight's rifle practice at Wimbledon, where the best prize of the year was won by his skill, he must return to the moors and covers for more deadly sport; and the calls of more important business, besides, required his presence in England. He paddled down the Rhine to Cologne, and on the way several times performed the difficult feat of hooking on his canoe to a steamer going at full speed.

Meantime, I had taken my boat up the Rhine by railway to Freyburg, from whence my real voyage was to begin, for as yet I had not paddled in parts unknown.

CHAPTER III.

Hollenthal Pass—Black Forest—Beds—Lake Titisee—
Storm—Source of the Danube.

PLANNING your summer tour is one of the most agreeable of occupations. It is in June or July that the Foreign Bradshaw becomes suddenly of intense interest, and the well-known pages of "Steamers and Railways"—why, it is worth while being a bachelor to be able to read each of these as part of your sketched-out plan, and (oh, selfish thought!) to have only one mind to consult as to whither away.

All this pleasure is a good deal influenced, however, by true answers to these questions,—Have you worked hard in working time, so as to be entitled to play in these playhours? Is this to be a vacation of refreshment, or an idle lounge and killing of time? Are you going off to rest, and to recruit delicate health, or with vigour to enjoy a summer of active exertion?

Bradshaw could not help me with the canoe one iota, and Baedeker was not written for a boat; so at Freyburg my plans resolved themselves into the simple direction, "Go at once to the source of the Danube."

Next morning, therefore, found the Rob Roy in a cart, and the grey-clothed traveller walking beside it on the dusty Höllenthal road. The gay, light-hearted exultation of being strong and well, and on a right errand, and with unknown things to do and places to see and people to meet, who can describe this?

But how easy it is at such times to be glad, and to think this is being "thankful." After moralizing for a few miles, a carriage full of English people overtook me, and soon we became companions. "The English are so distant, so silent, such *hauteur*, and gloomy distrust," forsooth! A false verdict, say I. The ladies carried me off through the very pretty glen, and the canoe on its cart trundled slowly after us behind, through the Höllenthal Pass, which is too seldom visited by travellers, who so often admire the spire of Freyburg (from the railway perhaps), passing it on their route to Switzerland.

This entrance to the Schwartzwald, or Black Forest, is a woody, rocky, and grim defile, with an excellent road, and good inns.

The villages are of wood, and there is a sawmill in every other house, giving a busy, wholesome sound, mellowed by the patter of the waterwheel. Further on, where tourists' scenery stops, it is a grand, dark-covered ocean of hills. The houses get larger and larger, and fewer and fewer, and nearly every one has a little chapel built alongside, with a wooden saint's image of life-size nailed on the gable end. One night I was in one of these huge domiciles, when all the servants and ploughboys came in, and half said, half sung, their prayers, in a whining but yet musical tone, and then retired for a hearty supper.

Our carriage mounted still among crags, bowing nearer to meet across the narrow gorge, and crested by the grand trees that will be felled and floated down the Rhine on one of those huge rafts you meet at Strasbourg. But everybody must have seen a Rhine raft, so I need not describe it, with its acres of wood and its street of cabin dwellings, and its gay coloured flags. A large raft needs 500 men to navigate it, and the timber of it sells for 30,000*l*.

At the top of this pass was the watershed of this first chain of hills, so my English friends took leave of me and returned. The Rob Roy was safely housed in the Baar Inn, and I set off for a long walk to find if the stream there would possibly be navigable.

Alone on a hillside in a foreign land, and with an evening sun on the wild mountains, there is a certain sense of independent delight that possesses the mind and being with a buoyant gladness; but how can I explain it in words, if you have not felt this sort of pleasure?

However, the rivulet was eminently unsuited for a canoe; so now let me go to bed in my wooden room, where the washingbasin is oval, and the partitions are so thin that one hears all the noises of the place at midnight. Now, the long-drawn snore of the landlord; then, the tittle-tattle of the servants not asleep yet, a pussy's plaintive mew, and the scraping of a mouse; the cows breathing in soft slumber; and, again, the sharp rattle of a horse's chain.

The elaborate construction of that edifice of housewifery called a "bett" here, and which we are expected to sleep upon, can only be understood when you have to undermine and dismantle it night after night to arrive at a reasonable flat surface on which to recline.

First you take off a great fluff bag, at least two feet thick, then a counterpane, and then a brilliant scarlet blanket; next you extract one enormous pillow, another enormous pillow, and a huge wedge-shaped bolster,—all, it appears, requisite for the Teutonic race, who yet could surely put themselves to sleep at an angle of forty-five degrees, without all this trouble, by merely tilting up the end of a flat bedstead.

Simple but real courtesy have I found throughout. Every one says "Gut tag;" and, even in a hotel, on getting up from breakfast a guest who has not spoken a word will wish "Gut morgen" as he departs, and perhaps "Bon appetit" to those not satisfied like himself. About eight o'clock the light repast of tea or coffee, bread, butter, and honey begins the day; at noon is the dinner, or "mittagessen," mid-day meal, giving all proper excuse for another dining operation in the shape of a supper at seven.

No fine manners here! My driver sat down to dinner with me, and the waiter along with him, smoking a cigar between whiles, as he waited on us both. But all this is just as one sees in Canada and in Norway, and wherever there are mountains, woods, and torrent streams, with a sparse population; and, as in Norway too, you see at once that all can read, and they do read. There is more reading in one day in a common house in Germany than in a month in the same sort of place in France.

I had hired the cart and driver by the day, but he by no means admired my first directions nex morning—namely, to take the boat off the main road, so as to get to the Titisee, a pretty mountain lake about four miles long, and surrounded by wooded knolls. His arguments and objections were evidently superficial, and something deeper than he said was in his mind. In fact, it appears that, by a **superstition long cherished there, Pontius Pilate is supposed to be in that deep, still lake, and** dark rumours were **told** that **he would** surely drag me down if **I ventured upon it.**

The legend about Pilate extends over Germany and Italy. Even on the flanks of Stromboli there is a *talus* of the volcano which the people dare not approach, " because of Pontius Pilate."

Of course, this decided the matter, and when I launched the Rob Roy from the pebbly shore in a **fine** foggy morning, and in full view of the inhabitants of the region (eight in number at last census), I had a most pleasant paddle for several miles.

At a distance the boat was invisible (being **so low in the water),** and they said that only a man was seen, whirling a paddle about his head.

There is nothing interesting about this lake, except that it is 3,000 feet above the sea and very **lonely,** in the middle of the Black Forest. Certainly no English boat has been there before, and probably no other will visit the deserted water.

After this, the Rob Roy is carted again still

further into the forests. Lumbering vehicles meet us, all carrying wood. Some have joined three carts together, and have eight horses. Others have a bullock or two besides, and all the men are intelligent enough, for they stop and stare, and my driver deigns to tell them, in a patois wholly beyond me, as to what a strange fare he has got with a boat and no other luggage. However, they invariably conclude that the canoe is being carried about for sale, and it could have been well sold frequently already.

About mid-day my sage driver began to mutter something at intervals, but I could only make out from his gestures and glances that it had to do with a storm overhead. The mixture of English, French, and German on the borders of the Rhine accustoms one to hear odd words. "Shall have you pottyto?" says a waiter, and he is asking if you will have potatoes. Another hands you a dish, saying, it is "sweetbone," and you must know it is "sweetbread."

Yes, the storm came, and as it seldom does come except in such places. I once heard a thunder peal while standing on the crater of Mount Vesuvius, and I have seen the grand beauty of bright lightning playing on the Falls of Niagara in a black dark night, but the vividness of the lightning to-day in the Black

Forest, and the crashing, rolling, and booming of the terrible and majestic battery of heaven was astounding. Once a bolt fell so near and with such a blaze that the horse (albeit tired enough) started off down a hill and made me quite nervous lest he should overturn the cart and injure my precious boat, which naturally was more and more dear to me as it was longer my sole companion.

As we toiled up the Rothenhaus Pass, down came the rain, whistling and rushing through the cold, dark forests of larch, and blackening the top of great Feldberg, the highest mountain here, and then pouring heavy and fast on the cart and horse, the man, the canoe, and myself. This was the last rain my boat got in the tour. All other days I spent in her were perfectly dry.

People stared out of their windows to see a cart and a boat in this heavy shower—what! a boat, up here in the hills? Where can it be going, and whose is it? Then they ran out to us, and forced the driver to harangue, and he tried to satisfy their curiosity, but his explanation never seemed to be quite exhaustive, for they turned homeward shaking their heads and looking grave, even though I nodded and laughed at them through the bars of the cart, lifting up my head among the wet straw.

The weather dried up its tears at last, and the

sun glittered on the road, still sparkling with its rivulets of rain water. The boat was soon cleared from wet by a sponge, while a smart walk warmed its well-soaked captain.

The horse too had got into a cheerful vein and actually trotted with excitement, for now it was down hill, and bright sun—a welcome change in ten minutes from our labouring up a steep forest road in a thunder-storm.

I suppose that the most rigid teetotaller (I am only a temperance man) would allow that just a very small glass of kirchwasser might be prescribed at this moment with advantage, and as there was no "faculty" there but myself, I administered the dose medicinally to the driver and to his employer, and gave a bran-mash and a rub down to the horse, which made all three of us better satisfied with ourselves and each other, and so we jogged on again.

By dusk I marched into Donaueschingen, and on crossing the little bridge, saw at once I could begin the Danube from its very source, for there were at least three inches of water in the middle of the stream.

In five minutes a crowd assembled round the boat, even before it could be loosened from the cart.*

* After trying various modes of securing the canoe in a springless cart for long journeys on rough and hilly

The ordinary idlers came first, then the more shy townspeople, and then a number of strange folks, whose exact position I could not make out, until it was explained that the great singing meeting for that part of Germany was to be held next day in the town, and so there were 600 visitors, all men of some means and intelligence, who were collected from a wide country round about.

The town was in gala for this meeting of song. The inns were full, but still the good landlord of the "Poste" by the bridge gave me an excellent room, and the canoe was duly borne in procession to the coachhouse.

What a din these tenors and basses did make at the table d'hôte! Everything about the boat had to be told a dozen times over to them, while my driver had a separate lecture-room on the subject below.

The town was well worth inspection next day, for it was in a violent fit of decoration.

---

roads, I am convinced that the best way is to fasten two ropes across the top of a long cart and let the boat lie on these, which will bear it like springs and so modify the jolts. The painter is then made fast fore and aft, so as to keep the boat from moving back and forward. All plans for using trusses of straw, &c., fail after a few miles of rolling gravel and coarse ruts.

E

Every house was tidied up, and all the streets were swept clean. From the humbler windows hung green boughs and garlands, rugs, quilts, and blankets; while banners, Venetian streamers, arches, mottoes, and wreaths of flowers announced the wealthier houses. Crowds of gaping peasants paraded the streets and jostled against bands drumming and tromboning (if there be such a word), and marching in a somewhat ricketty manner over the undoubtedly rough pavement. Every now and then the bustle had a fresh paroxysm when four horses rattled along, bringing in new visitors from some distant choir. They are coming you see in a long four-wheeled cart, covered with evergreens and bearing four pine trees in it erect among sacks which are used as seats—only the inmates do not sit but stand up in the cart and shout, and sing, and wave banners aloft, while the hundreds of on-lookers roar out the "Hoch," the German Hurrah! with only one note.

As every window had its ornament or device, I made one for mine also, and my sails were festooned (rather tastefully, I flatter myself) to support the little blue silk English jack of the canoe. This complimentary display was speedily recognized by the Germans, who greeted it with cheers, and sung glees below, and improvised

ALLEGRO. 51

Singers' Waggon.

verses about England, and then sang round the boat itself, laughing, shouting, and hurraing boisterously with the vigour of youthful lungs. Never tell me again that the Germans are a phlegmatic people!

They had a "banket" in the evening at the Museum. It was "free for all," and so 400 came on these inexpensive terms, and all drank beer from long glass cylinders at a penny a glass, all smoked cigars at a farthing a piece, and all talked and sung, though a splendid brass band was playing beside them, and whenever it stopped a glee or chorus commenced.

The whole affair was a scene of bewildering excitement, very curious to contemplate for one sitting in the midst. Next me I found a young bookseller who had sold me a French book in the morning. He said I must take a ticket for the Sunday concert; but I told him I was an Englishman, and had learned in my country that it was God's will and for men's good to keep Sunday for far better things, which are too much forgotten when one day in seven is not saved from the business, excitement, and giddiness of every-day life.

There is a feeling of dull sameness about life in those countries and places where the week is not steadied and centered round a solid day on which lofty and deep things, pure and lasting things may have at least some hours of our attention.

So I left the merry singers to bang their drums and hoch! at each other in the great hall provided for their use by the Prince of Furstemburg. He had reared this near his stables, in which are many good horses, some of the best being English, and named on their stalls "Miss," "Pet," "Lady," or "Tom," &c.

An English gentleman whom I met afterwards had been travelling through Germany with a four-in-hand drag, and he came to Donaueschingen, where the Prince soon heard of his arrival. Next day His Serene Highness was at his stables, and seeing an English visitor there, he politely conducted the stranger over the whole establishment, explaining every item with minute care. He found out afterwards that this visitor was not the English gentleman, but only his groom!

The intelligence, activity, and good temper of most of the German waiters in hotels will surely be observed by travellers whose daily enjoyment depends so much on that class. Here, for instance, is a little waiter at the Poste Inn. He is the size of a boy, but looks twenty years older. His face is flat, and broad, and brown, and so is his jacket. His shoulders are high, and he reminds you of those four everlasting German juveniles, with thick comforters about their necks, who stand in London streets blowing brass music, with their cheeks puffed out, and their cold grey eyes turning on all the passing objects while the music, or at any rate a noise, blurts out as if mechanically from the big, unpolished instruments held by red benumbed fingers.

This waiter lad then is all day at the beck of all, and never gets a night undisturbed, yet he is as obliging at ten o'clock in the dark as for the early coffee at sunrise, and he quite agrees with each guest, in the belief that *his* particular cutlet or cognac is the most important feature of the hour.

I honour this sort of man. He fills a hard place well, and Bismarck or Mussurus cannot do more.

Then again, there is Ulric, the other waiter, hired only for to-day as an "extra," to meet the crush of hungry vocalists who will soon fill the *saal*. He is timid yet, being young, and only used to a village inn where "The Poste at Donaueschingen" is looked up to with solemn admiration as the pink of fashion. He was learning French too, and was sentimental, so I gave him a very matter-of-fact book, and then he asked me to let him sit in the canoe while I was to paddle it down the river to his home! The naïve simplicity of this request was truly refreshing, and if I had been sure of shallow water all the way, and yet not too shallow, it would perhaps have been amusing to admit such a passenger.

The actual source of the Danube is by no means agreed upon any more than the source of the Nile. I had a day's exploration of the country, after seeking exact information on this point from the townspeople in vain. The land round Donaueschingen is a spongy soil, with numerous rivulets and a few large streams. I went along one of these, the Brege, which rises twenty miles away, near St. Martin, and investigated about ten miles of another, the Brigach, a brook rising near St. Georgen, about a mile from the source of the Neckar, which river runs to the Rhine. These streams join near Donaueschingen, but in the town there bubbles up a clear spring of water in the gardens of the Prince near the church, and this, the infant Danube, runs into the other water already wide enough for a boat, but which then for the first time has the name of Donau.

The name, it is said, is never given to either of the two larger rivulets, because sometimes both have been known to fail in dry summers, while the bubbling spring has been perennial for ages.

The Brege and another confluent are caused to fill an artificial pond close by the Brigach. This lake is wooded round, and has a pretty island, and swans, and gold fish. A waterwheel (in vain covered for concealment) pumps up water to flow from an inverted horn amid a group of statuary in this romantic pond, and the stream flowing from it also joins the others.

That there might be no mistake however in this matter, I went on each stream from the first point where it would float a canoe, and while the **singers** *sol-faed* excessively at the boat, and shouted hochs and farewells to the English "flagge," and the landlord bowed (his bill of thirteen francs for three full days being duly paid), and the **populace** stared, the Rob Roy shot off like an arrow on a river delightfully new.

CHAPTER IV.

The Danube—Singers—Shady nooks—Geislingen—Morning Crowd—Islands—Monks—Concert—Fish—A race.

AT first the river is a few feet broad, but it soon enlarges, and the streams of a great plain quickly bring its volume to that of the Thames at Kingston. The Donau (old Roman Ister) winds about then in serpentine slowness and smoothness for hours in a level mead, with waving sedge on the banks and silken sleepy weeds in the water. Here the long-necked, long-winged, long-legged heron, that seems to have forgotten to get a body, flocks by scores with ducks of the various wild breeds, while pretty painted butterflies and fierce-looking dragon-flies float, as it were, on the summer sunbeams, and simmer in the air. The haymakers are at work; and half their work is hammering the soft edges of their very miserable scythes, which they then dip in the water; now they have a chat; and as I whiz by round a corner, there is a row of open mouths and wondering eyes, but an immediate return to courtesy with a touch of the hat, and "Gut tag" when presence of mind is restored. Then they call to their mates, and laugh with rustic satisfaction—a laugh that is real and true, not cynical, but the recognition of a strange incongruity, that of a reasonable being pent up in a boat and hundreds of miles from home, yet whistling most cheerfully all the time!

Soon the hills on either side have houses and old castles, and then wood, and, lastly, rock; and with these, mingling the bold, the wild, and the sylvan, there begins a grand panorama of river beauties to be unrolled for days and days. No river I have seen equals this Upper Danube, and I have visited many pretty streams. The wood is so thick, the rocks so quaint and high and so much varied, the water is so clear, and the grass so green. Winding here and turning there, and rushing fast down this reach and paddling slow along that, with each minute a fresh view, and of new things, the mind is ever on the *qui vive*, or the boat will go bump on a bank, crash on a rock, or plunge into a tree full of gnats and spiders. This is veritable travelling, where skill and tact are needed to bear you along, and where each exertion of either is rewarded at once. I think, also, it promotes decision of character, for you *must* choose, and that promptly, too, between, say, five channels opened suddenly before you. Three are probably safe, but which of these three is the shortest, deepest, and most practicable? In an instant, if you hesitate, the boat is on a bank; and it is remarkable how speedily the exercise of this resolution becomes experienced into habit, but of course only after some severe lessons.

It is exciting to direct a camel over the sandy desert when you have lost your fellow-travellers, and to guide a horse in trackless wilds alone; but the pleasure of paddling a canoe down a rapid, high-banked, and unknown river, is far more than these.

Part of this pleasure flows from the mere sense of rapid motion. In going down a swift reach of the river there is the same sensation about one's diaphragm which is felt when one goes forward smoothly on a lofty rope swing. Now the first few days of the Danube are upon very fast waters. Between its source and Ulm the descent of the river is about 1,500 feet.* This would give 300 feet of fall for each of a five days' journey; and it will be seen from this that the prospect for the day's voyage is most cheering

* The best geographical books give different estimates of this, some above and others below the amount here stated.

when you launch in the morning and know you will have to descend about the height of St. Paul's Cathedral before halting for the night.

Another part of the pleasure—it is not to be denied—consists in satisfaction at overcoming difficulties. When you have followed a channel chosen from several, and, after half-a-mile of it, you see one and another of the rejected channels emerging from its islands to join that you are in, there is a natural pride in observing that any other streamlet but the one you had chosen would certainly have been a mistake.

These reflections are by the way; and we have been winding the while through a rich grassy plain till a bridge over the river made it seem quite a civilized spot, and, just as I passed under, there drove along one of the green-boughed waggons of jovial singers returning from Donaueschingen. Of course they recognised the canoe, and stopped to give her a hearty cheer, ending with a general chorus made up of the few English words of their vocabulary, "All r-r-r-r-ight, Englishmánn!" "All r-r-r-r-ight, Englishmánn!" *

The coincidence of these noisy but good-humoured people having been assembled in the morning, when the canoe had started from the

* See sketch, *ante,* page 51.

source of the Danube, caused the news of its adventure to be rapidly carried to all the neighbouring towns, so that the Rob Roy was welcomed at once, and the newspapers recorded its proceedings not only in Germany and France, but in England, and even in Sweden and in America.

At the village of Geislingen I discovered that the boiler of my engine needed some fuel, or, in plain terms, I must breakfast. The houses of the town were not close to the river, but some workmen were near at hand, and I had to leave the canoe in the centre of the stream moored to a plank, with very strict injunctions (in most distinct English!) to an intelligent boy to take charge of her until my return; and then I walked to the principal street, and to the best-looking house, and knocked, entered, asked for breakfast, and sat down, and was speedily supplied with an excellent meal. One after another the people came in to look at the queer stranger who was clad so oddly, and had come—aye, *how* had he come? that was what they argued about in whispers till he paid his bill, and then they followed to see where he would go, and thus was there always a congregation of inquisitive but respectful observers as we started anew.

Off again, though the August sun is hot.

Shade will be better enjoyed when resting in the boat under a high rock, or in a cool water cave, or beneath a wooden bridge, or within the longer shadow of a pine-clad cliff.

Often I tried to rest those midday hours (for one cannot always work) on shore, in a house, or on a grassy bank; but it was never so pleasant as at full length in the canoe, under a thick grown oak-tree, with a book to read dreamily, and a mild cigar at six for a penny, grown in the fields I passed, and made up at yesterday's inn.*

---

* Two stimulants well known in England are much used in Germany,—tea and tobacco.

(1) The tobacco plant (sometimes styled a weed, because it also grows wild) produces leaves, which are dried and rolled, and then treated with fire, using an appropriate instrument, by which the fumes are inhaled. The effect upon many persons is to soothe; but it impairs the appetite of others. The use is carried to excess in Turkey. The leaves contain a deadly poison.

(2) The tea weed (sometimes styled a plant, because it also grows under cultivation) produces leaves, which are dried and rolled, and then treated with fire, using an appropriate instrument, by which the infusion is imbibed. The effect upon many persons is to cheer; but it impairs the sleep of others. The use is carried to excess in Russia. The leaves contain a deadly poison.

Both these luxuries are cheap and portable, especially tobacco, and are daily enjoyed by millions of persons in all

Let it be well understood that this picture only describes the resting time, and not the active hours of progress in the cooler part of the day before and after the bright meridian sun.

In working hours there was no lazy lolling, the enjoyment was that of delightful exertion, varied at every reach of the river, and never two hours alike all the way through.

You start, indeed, quietly enough, but are sure soon to hear the well-known rushing sound of a milldam, and this almost every day, five or six times. On coming to it I usually went straight along the top edge of the weir, looking over for a good place to descend by, and surveying the innumerable little streams below to see my best course afterwards. By this time the miller and his family and his men, and all the neighbours, would run down to see the new sight, but I always lifted out my little black knapsack and put my paddle on shore, and then stepped out and pulled my boat over or round the obstruction, sometimes through a hayfield or two, or by a lane, or along a wall, and then launched her again in deep water. Dams less than four feet

climates. Both also require care and moderation in their use. Both have advocates and enemies; and it cannot be settled by argument whether the plant or the weed is the most useful to mankind.

high one can "shoot" with a headlong plunge into the little billows at the foot, but this wrenches the boat if it strikes against a stone, and it is better to get out and ease her through, lift her over, or drag her round.

In other places I had to sit **astride on the** stern of the canoe, with both legs in the **water,** fending her off from big stones on either **side,** and cautiously steering.*

But with these amusements, and a little wading, you sit quite dry, and, leaning against the backboard, smoothly glide past every danger, lolling at ease where the current is excessive, and **where it** would not be safe to **add** impetus, for the **shock** of a collision there **would** break the strongest boat.

If incidents like these, and the scenery and **the** people ashore, **were not** enough to satisfy **the ever** greedy mind, some louder plashing, with a deeper roar, would announce the rapids. This sound was sure to waken up any sleepiness, and once in the middle of rough water all had to be energy and life.

I never had a positive upset, but of course I

* **The** invention of this method was made here, but its invaluable advantages were more apparent in passing the second rapid of Rheinfelden. See *post*, page 189, where it is described, with a sketch.

had to jump out frequently to save the boat, for the first care was the canoe, and the second was my luggage, to keep it all dry, the sketch-book in particular, while the third object was to get on comfortably and fast.

After hours of these pleasures of work and rest, and a vast deal seen and heard and felt that would take too long to tell, the waning sun, and the cravings within for dinner, warned me truly that I had come near the stopping-place for the night.

The town of Tuttlingen is built on both sides of the river, and almost every house is a dyer's shop or a tannery, with men beating, scraping, and washing hides in the water. As I allowed the boat to drift among these the boys soon found her out—a new object—and therefore to boys (and may it always be so) well worth a shout and a run; so a whole posse of little Germans scampered along beside me, but I could not see any feasible-looking inn.

It is one of the privileges of this water tour that you can survey calmly all the whereabouts; and being out of reach of the touters and porters who tyrannically oppress the wretched traveller delivered to their grasp from an omnibus or a steamboat, you can philosophize on the whole *morale* of a town, and if so inclined can pass it, and simply go on. In fact, on several occasions

I did not fancy a town, and so went on to another. However, I was fairly nonplussed now. It would not do to go further, for it was not a thickly-peopled country; but I went nearly to the end of the place in search of a good landing, till I turned into a millrace and stepped ashore.

The crowd pressed so closely that I had to fix on a boy who had a toy barrow with four little wheels, and amid much laughter I persuaded him to lend it (of course as a great honour to him), and so I pulled the boat on this to the hotel. The boy's sixpence of reward was a fact that brought all the juvenile population together, and though I hoisted the canoe into a hayloft and gave very positive injunction to the ostler to keep her safe, there was soon a string of older sight-seers admitted one by one; and even at night they were mounting the ladder with lanterns, women as well as men, to examine the " schiff."

A total change of garments usually enabled me to stroll through the villages in the evening without being recognised, but here I was instantly known as I emerged for a walk, and it was evident that an unusual attendance must be expected in the morning.

Tuttlingen is a very curious old town, with a good inn and bad pavement, tall houses, all leaning here and there, and big, clumsy, honest-

MORNING VISITORS.

looking men lounging after their work, and wonderfully satisfied to chat in groups amid the signal darkness of unlighted streets; very fat horses and pleasant-looking women, a bridge, and numerous schoolboys; these are my impressions of Tuttlingen.

Even at six o'clock next morning these boys had begun to assemble for the sight they expected, and those of them who had satchels on their backs seemed grievously disappointed to find the start would not come off before their hour for early school.

However, the grown-up people came instead, and flocked to the bridge and its approaches. While I was endeavouring to answer all the usual questions as to the boat, a man respectfully asked me to delay the start five minutes, as his aged father, who was bedridden, wished exceedingly just to see the canoe. In all such cases it is a pleasure to give pleasure, and to sympathize with the boundless delight of the boys, remembering how as a boy a boat delighted me; and then, again, these worthy, mother-like, wholesome-faced dames, how could one object to their prying gaze, mingled as it was with friendly smiles and genuine interest?

The stream on which I started here was not the main channel of the Danube, but a narrow arm of the river conducted through the town, while the other part fell over the mill-weir. The woodcut shows the scene at starting, but there were crowds as large as this at other towns; and a picture never can repeat the shouts and bustle, or the sound of guns firing and bells ringing, which on more than one occasion celebrated the Rob Roy's morning paddle.

The lovely scenery of this day's voyage often reminded me of that upon the Wye,* in its best parts between Ross and Chepstow. There were the white rocks and dark trees, and caverns, crags, and jutting peaks you meet near Tintern; but then the Wye has no islands, and its muddy water at full tide has a worse substitute in muddier banks when the sea has ebbed.

The islands on beauteous Donau were of all sizes and shapes. Some low and flat, and thickly covered with shrubs; others of stalwart rock, stretching up at a sharp angle, under which the glassy water bubbled all fresh and clear.

Almost each minute there was a new scene,

* Murray says: "The Meuse has been compared to the Wye; but is even more romantic than the English river." I would rank the Wye as much above the Meuse as below the Danube for romance in scenery.

and often I backed against the current to hold my post in the best view of some grand picture. Magnificent crags reached high up on both sides, and impenetrable forests rung with echoes when I shouted in the glee of health, freedom, and exquisite enjoyment.

But scenes and sentiments will not feed the hungry paddler, so I decided to stop at Freidingen, a village on the bank. There was a difficulty now as to where I could leave the canoe, for no inn seemed near enough to let me guard her while I breakfasted. At length a mason helped me to carry the Rob Roy into a donkey's stable, and a boy volunteered to guide the stranger to the best inn. The first, and the second, and the third he led me to were all beerhouses, where only drink could be had; and, as the crowd augmented at every stage, I dismissed the ragged cicerone, and trusted (as I ought to have done at first) to that unnamed instinct which guides a hungry man to food. Even the place I found at last, was soon filled with wondering spectators. A piece of a German and English dictionary from my baggage excited universal attention, and was several times carried outside to those who had not secured reserved seats within.

The magnificent scenery culminated at Beuron, where a great convent on a rich mound of grass is nearly surrounded by the Danube, amid a spacious amphitheatre of cliffs perfectly upright, and clad with the heaviest wood.

The place looked so lonely, though fair, that I could scarcely believe I was to stop there for the night, and so I had nearly swept by it again into perfect solitude when at last I pulled up under a tree, and walked through well ploughed fields to the little hamlet in this sequestered spot.

The field labourers were of course surprised at the apparition of a man in flannel, who must have come out of the river; but the people at the Kloster had already heard of the "schiff," and the Rob Roy was soon mounted on two men's shoulders, and borne in triumph to the excellent hotel. The Prince who founded the monastery is, I believe, himself a monk.

Now tolls the bell for "even song," while my dinner is spread in an arbour looking out on this grand scene, made grander still by dark clouds gathering on the mountains, and a loud and long thunder peal, with torrents of rain.

This deluge of wet came opportunely when I had such good shelter, as it cooled the air, and would strengthen the stream of the river; so I admired the venerable monks with complacent satisfaction, a feeling never so complete as when you are inside, and you look at people who are out in the rain.

A young girl on a visit to her friends here could talk bad French rapidly, so she was sent to gossip with me as I dined; and then the whole family inspected my sketch-book, a proceeding which happened at least twice every day for many weeks of the voyage. This emboldened me to ask for some music, and the whole party adjourned to a great hall, where a concert was soon in progress with a guitar, a piano, and a violin, all well played; and the Germans are never at a loss for a song.

My young visitor, Melanie, then became the interpreter in a curious conversation with the others, who could speak only German; and I ventured to turn our thoughts on some of the nobler things which ought not to be long absent from the mind—I mean, what is loved and feared, enjoyed and derided, as "religion."

In my very limited baggage I had brought some selected pieces and Scripture anecdotes and other papers in French and German, and these were used on appropriate occasions, and were always well received, often with exceedingly great interest and sincere gratitude.

Some people are shy about giving tracts, or are even afraid of them. But then some people are shy of speaking at all, or even dislike to ride, or skate, or row. One need not laugh at another for this.

The practice of carrying a few printed pages to convey in clear language what one cannot accurately speak in a foreign tongue is surely allowable, to say the least. But I invariably find it to be very useful and interesting to myself and to others; and, as it hurts nobody, and has nothing in it of which to be proud or ashamed, and as hundreds of men do it, and as I have done it for years, and will do it again, I am far too old a traveller to be laughed out of it now.

The Kloster at Beuron is a favourite place for excursionists from the towns in the neighbourhood, and no doubt some day soon it will be a regular "place to see" for English travellers rowing down the Danube; for it is thus, and only thus, you can approach it with full effect. The moon had come out as I looked from my bedroom window, and it whitened the ample circus of beetling crags, and darkened the trees, while a fainter and redder light glimmered from the monks' chapel, as the low tones of midnight chanting now and then reached the ear. Perhaps it is better to wear a monk's cowl than to wear consistently a layman's common coat in the workday throng of life; and it *may* be better to fast and chant and kneel at shrines than to be temperate and thankful and prayerful in the busy world. But I doubt.

After leaving Beuron, with the usual pleasant good wishes from the shore, the Danube carried us between two lofty rocks, and down calm reaches for hours. The water was unspeakably clear; you could see right into deep caverns far below. I used to gaze downwards for so long a time at the fish moving about, and to strike at them with my long paddle (never once hitting any), that I forgot that the boat was swinging along all the time, till bump she went on a bank, or crash against a rocky isle, or rumbling into some thick trees, when a shower of leaves, spiders, and rubbish would waken up my reverie. Then, warned by the shock, I return to the plain duty of looking ahead, until, perhaps, after an hour's active rushing through narrow "guts," and over little falls, and getting out and hauling the boat down larger ones, my eyes are wandering again, gazing at the peaks overhead, and at the eagles soaring above them, and at the clear blue sky above all; till again the Rob Roy heels over on a sunken stone, and I have to jump out nimbly to save her from utter destruction. For days together I had my feet bare, and my trousers tucked up, ready to wade at any moment, and perfectly comfortable all the time, for a fiery sun dried every thing in a few minutes.

The physical enjoyment of such a life to one in good health and good spirits, with a good boat and good scenery, is only to be appreciated after experience; for these little reminders, that one must not positively sleep on a rushing river, never resulted in any disaster, and I came home without a cold or a scratch, or a hole in the boat, or one single day regretted. May this be so for many a John Bull let loose on the Continent to "paddle his own canoe."

On the rivers, where there is no navigation and no towing-paths, it was impossible to estimate the distances traversed each day, except by the number of hours I was at work, the average speed, the strength of the wind and current, and the number of stoppages for food or rest, or mill-weirs, waterfalls, or barriers. I reckoned thirty miles to be a good day's work, and I have sometimes gone forty miles in a day; but I was content with twenty when the scenery and incidents on the way filled up every moment of time with varied sensations of new pleasures.

It will generally be found, I think, that for walking in a pleasant country twenty miles a day is enough for mind and body, to be active and observant all the time. But the events that occur in river work are far more frequent and interesting than those on the road, for you have all the circumstances of your boat in addition to what fills the pedestrian's journal, and after a little time your canoe becomes so much a companion (friend, shall I say?) that every turn it takes and every knock and grate on its side is felt as if it were your own. The boat gets to be individualized, and so does the river, till at last there is a pleasant rivalry set up, for it is "man and boat" *versus* the river and all it can place in your way.

After a few tours on the Continent your first hour in a railway or diligence may be new and enjoyable, but you soon begin to wish for the end of the road, and after a short time in the town you have come to you begin to talk (or think) of when you are to leave. Now a feature of the boating tour is that quiet progress can be enjoyed all the time, because you have personal exertion or engagement for every moment, and your observation of the scenery around is far more minute and interesting, because every bend and slope of it tells at once on what you have to do.

Certainly the pleasure of a day is not to be measured by the number of miles you have gone over. The voyage yesterday, for instance, was one of the very best for enjoyment of scenery, incident, and exercise, yet it was the shortest day I had. The guide-book says, "Tuttlingen is twelve miles"—by river, say eighteen—"from Kloster Beuron, where the fine scenery begins. This part of the Danube is not navigable."

I will not say that on some occasions I did not wish for the end of the day's work, when arms were weary, and the sun was low, and yearnings of the inner man grumbled for dinner, especially when no one could tell how far it was to any house, or whether you could stop there all night if you reached it.

CHAPTER V.

Sigmaringen—Treacherous trees—Congress of herons—
Flying Dutchman—**Tub** and shovel—Bottle race—
Snags—Ya Vol—Benighted.

THE sides of the river were now less precipitous, and the road came within a field or two of the water, and made it seem quite homely for a time.

I had heard a loud jingling sound on this road for at least half-an-hour, and observed a long cart with two horses trotting fast, and evidently, as I thought, daring to race with the Rob Roy. But at length such earnest signals were made from it that I stopped, and the cart at once pulled up, and there ran across the field a man breathless and hot, without his hat, and followed by two young ladies, equally hurried. He was a German, resident for a short time in London, and now at home for a month's holiday, and he was prodigal of thanks for my "great courtesy" in having stopped that the ladies might see the canoe which they had followed thus for some miles, having heard of its fame at their village. On another occasion three youths voluntarily ran alongside the boat and panted in the sun, and tumbled over stocks and stones at such a rate, that after a mile of the supererogatory exercise, I asked what it was all about. Excellent villagers! they had taken all this trouble to arrive at a point farther down the stream where they knew there was a hard place, and they thought they might help me in passing it.

Such exertions on behalf of a stranger were really most kind, and when I allowed them to give a nominal help, where in reality it was easy enough to get on unaided, they were much delighted and more than rewarded, and went back prattling their purest Suabian in a highly satisfied frame of mind.

Many are the bends and currents, but at last we arrive at the town of Sigmaringen. It has certainly an aristocratic air, though there are only 3,000 inhabitants; but then it has a Principality, though the whole population of this is only 52,000. Fancy a parish in London having a Prince all to themselves, and with such a fine grand name too—" His Royal Serene Highness the Hereditary Prince of Hohenzollern Sigmaringen." But though I have often laughed at this petty kingdom in the Geography books, I shall never do so again, for it contains some of the most beautiful river scenery in the world, and I never had more unalloyed pleasure in passing through a foreign dominion.

There are pretty gardens here, and a handsome Protestant church, and a few good shops, schlosses on the hills, and older castles perched on high rocks in the usual picturesque and uncomfortable places where our ancestors built their nests.

The Deutscher Hof is the hotel just opened three weeks ago, and all its inmates are in a flutter when their first English guest marches up to the door with a boat and a great company of gazers. The waiter too, all fresh from a year in London, at the Palace Hotel, Buckingham Gate, how glad he is that his English is now in requisition, sitting by me at dinner and talking most sensibly all the time.

The weather still continued superb; there was not a drop of rain yet, though I had not brought an umbrella. Deep green woods dipped their lower branches in the water, but I found that the stream had sometimes a fashion of carrying the boat under these, and it is especially needful to guard against this when a sharp bend with a fast current hurries you into a wooded corner. Indeed, strange as it may seem, there was more danger to the boat from these trees than from rocks or banks, and far more trouble. For when the boat gets under their low branches your paddle is quite powerless, because you cannot lower one end to hold the water without raising the other and so catching it in the trees. Then if you put your head down forward you cannot see, and the boughs are generally as hard as an ordinary skull when the two are in collision. Finally, if you lean backwards the twigs scrape your face and catch upon a nose even of ordinary length, and if you take your hand from the paddle to protect the face away goes the paddle into the river. Therefore, although my hat was never knocked off, and my skull was always the hardest, and my paddle was never lost, and my nose was never de-Romanized by the branches, I set it down as a maxim, to keep clear of trees in a stream.

Still it was tempting to go under shady groves when I tried to surprise a flock of herons or a family of wild ducks. Once I came upon twenty-four herons all together. As my boat advanced silently, steadily, it was curious to watch these birds, who had certainly never been disturbed before by any boat in such a place.

They stared eagerly at me and then looked at each other, and evidently took a vote of the assembly as to what all this could mean. If birds' faces can have an expression of opinion, I am sure I saw one of these saying then to the others

"Did you ever?" and an indignant sneer was on another's beak that plainly answered, "Such impudence indeed!" while a third added, with a sarcastic chirp, "And a foreigner too!" But, after consultation, they always got up and circled round, flew down stream, and then settled all again together in an adjourned meeting. A few minutes brought me to their new retreat, and so we went on for miles, they always flying down stream, and always assembling, though over and over again disturbed, until an amendment on the plan was moved and they bent their way aside.

A pleasant and favourable breeze springing up, which soon freshened into a gale, I now set my two sails, and the boat went with very great speed; dashing over rocks and bounding past the hayfields so fast that when one who caught sight of her had shouted to the rest of his "mates," the sight was departed for ever before they came, and I heard them behind me arguing, probably about the ghost.

But it was a shame to be a phantom ship too often, and it was far more amusing to go right into the middle of these people, who knew nothing about the canoe, who had never seen a boat, and never met a foreigner in their lives. Thus, when I found a waterfall too high to "shoot," or a wide barrier made it advisable to take the boat by land,

"In the Hayfields."

I used to walk straight into the hayfields, pushing the boat point foremost through a hedge, or dragging her steadily over the wet newly-mown grass in literal imitation of the American craft which could go "wherever there was a heavy dew." On such occasions the amazement of the untaught clowns, beholding suddenly such an apparition, was beyond all description. Some even ran away, very often children cried outright, and when I looked gravely on the ground as I marched and dragged the boat, and then suddenly stopped in their midst with a hearty laugh and an address in English, the whole proceeding may have appeared to them at least as strange as it did to me.

The water of the river all at once became here of a pale white colour, and I was mourning that my pretty scenes below were clouded; but in about thirty miles the pebbly deeps appeared again, and the stream resumed its charming limpid clearness. This matter of dark or bright water is of some importance, because, when it is clear, by a little experience you can easily estimate the general depth, even at some distance, by the shades and hues of the water, while the sunk rocks, big stones, and other particular obstacles are of course more visible then.

Usually I got well enough fed at some village, or at least at a house, but in this lonely part of the river it seemed wise to take provender with me in the boat, and to picnic in some quiet pool, with a shady tree above. One of the very few boats I saw on the river appeared as I was thus engaged, and a little boy was in it. His specimen of naval architecture (no doubt the only one he had ever seen) was an odd contrast to the beautifully finished canoe made by Searle. He had a pole and a shovel; the latter article he used as a paddle, and his boat was of enormous thickness and clumsiness, made of three planks, abundantly clamped with iron. I gave him some bread, and we had a chat; then some butter, and then some cheese. He would not take wine, but he produced a cigar from his wet jacket, and also two matches, which he lighted with great skill. We soon got to be friends, as people do who are together alone, and in the same mode of travelling, riding, or sailing, or on camels' backs. So we smiled in sympathy, and I asked him if he could read, and gave him a neat little page prettily printed in German, with a red border. This he read very nicely and was glad to put in his ragged pocket; but he could scarcely part from me, and struggled vainly to urge his tub along with the shovel till we came to a run of dashing waves, and then of course I had to leave him behind, looking and yearning, with a low, murmuring sound, and a sorrowful, earnest gaze I shall never forget.

Shoals of large and small fish are in this river, and very few fishermen. I did not see ten men fishing in ten days. But the pretty little Kingfisher does not neglect his proper duties, and ever and anon his round blue back shines in the sun as he hurries away with a note of protest against the stranger who has invaded his preserves. Bees are buzzing while the sun is hot, and when it sinks, out gush the endless mazes of gnats to hop and flit their tangled dances, the creatures of a day—born since the morning, and to die at night.

Before the Danube parted with the rocks that

had been on each side for days together, it played some strange pranks among them, and they with it.

Often they rose at each side a hundred feet without a bend, and then behind these were broken cliffs heaved this way and that, or tossed upside down, or as bridges hanging over chasms.

Here and there a huge splinted tooth-like spire of stone stuck out of the water, leaning at an angle. Sometimes in front there was a veritable upright wall, as smooth as if it were chiselled, and entirely cutting off the middle of the stream. In advancing steadily to such a place it was really impossible to decide on which side the stream could by any means find an exit, and once indeed I was persuaded that it must descend below.

In other cases the river, which had splayed out its width to that of the Thames at Hungerford, narrowed its size to a six-foot passage, and rushed down that with a " whishhh ! " A more difficult vagary to cope with was when in a dozen petty streams the water tumbled over as many little cascades, and only one was passable—sometimes not one. The interest of finding these, examining, trying, failing, and succeeding, was a continuous delight, and filled up every mile with a series of exciting incidents, till at length the rocks were done.

And now we enter a vast plain, with the stream bending round on itself, and hurrying swiftly on through the innumerable islands, eddies, and "snags," or trees uprooted, sticking in the water. At the most critical part of this labyrinth I was going a tremendous pace, when I suddenly came to a fork in the river, with the volumes of water going down both channels nearly equal. We could not descend by one of these because a tree would catch the mast, so I instantly turned into the other, when up started a man and shouted impetuously that no boat could pass by *that* course. It was a moment of danger, but I lowered the sails in that moment, took down my mast, and, despite stream and gale, I managed to paddle back to the proper channel. As I had not seen a man for hours before, the arrival of this warning note was opportune.

A new amusement was invented to-day—it was to pitch out my empty wine-bottle and to watch its curious bobbings and whirlings as the current carried it along, while I floated near and compared the natural course taken by the bottle with the selected route which intelligence gave to the Rob Roy. Soon the bottle became impersonated, and we were racing together, and yet a friendship began for its well-known cork as it plumped down when its bottom struck a stone—for the bottle drew more water than my canoe—and every time it grounded there came a loud and melancholy clink of the glass, and **down** it went.

The thick bushes near the river skirted it now for miles, and at one place I could see above me, through the upper branches, **about 20 haymakers, men and women,** who were honestly working away, and therefore had not observed **my approach.**

I resolved to have a bit of fun here, so I closed in **to the** bank, but still so as to see the industrious group. Then suddenly I began in a very loud voice with—

"Rule, Britannia,
Britannia rules the waves."

Long before I got to the word "slaves" the whole party were like statues, silent and fixed in amazement. Then they looked right, left, before, behind, and upwards in all directions, except, **of course,** into the river, for why should they look *there?* nothing had ever come up from the river to disturb their quiet mead. I next whistled a lively air, and then dashing out of my hiding-place stood up in my boat, and made a brief (but, I trust, brilliant) speech to them in the best English I could muster, and in a moment afterwards I had vanished from their sight.

A little farther on there was some road-making in progress, and I pulled up my boat under a tree and walked up to the "barraque," or workman's canteen, and entered among 30 or 40 German "navvies," who were sitting at their midday beer. I ordered a glass and drank their health standing, paid, bowed, and departed, but a general rush ensued to see where on earth this flannel-clad being had come from, and they stood on the bank in a row as I waded, shoved, hauled, paddled, and carried my boat through a troublesome labyrinth of channels and embankments, with which their engineering had begun to spoil the river.

But the bridges one had now more frequently to meet were far worse encroachments of civilization, for most of them were so low that my mast would not pass under without heeling the boat over to one side, so as to make the mast lean over obliquely. In one case of this kind she was very nearly shipwrecked. The wind was so good that I would not lower the sail, and this and a swift current took us (me and my boat—she is now, you see, installed as a "person") rapidly to the centre arch, when just as we entered I noticed a fierce-looking snag with a sharp point exactly in my course. To swerve to the side would be to strike the wooden pier, but even this would be better (for I might ward off the violence of a blow near my hands) than to run on the snag, which would be certain to cut a hole.

With a heavy thump on the pier the canoe began to capsize, and only by the nearest escape was she saved from foundering. What I thought was a snag turned out to be the point of an iron stake or railing, carelessly thrown into the water from the bridge above.

It may be remarked here that many hidden dangers occur near bridges, for there are wooden or iron bars fixed under water, or rough sharp stones lying about, which, being left there when the bridge was building, are not removed from a river not navigable or used by boats.

Another kind of obstruction is the thin wire rope suspended across the rivers, where a ferry is established by running a flat boat over the stream with cords attached to the wire rope. This rope is black in colour, and therefore not noticed till you approach it too near to lower the mast, but this sort of danger is easily avoided by the somewhat sharp "look-out" which a week or two on the water makes quite instinctive and habitual. Perhaps one of the many advantages of a river tour is the increased acuteness of observation which it requires and fosters.

I stopped next at a clumsy sort of town called

Reidlingen, where an Englishman is a very rare visitor. The excitement here about the boat became almost ridiculous, and one German, who had been in America and could jabber a little in my language, was deputed to ask questions, while the rest heard the answers interpreted.

Next morning at eight o'clock at least a thousand people gathered on the bridge and its approaches to see the boat start, and shoals of schoolboys ran in, each with his little knapsack of books.*

The scenery after this became of only ordinary interest compared with what I had passed through, but there would have been little spare time to look at it had it been ever so picturesque, for the wind was quite a gale,† and right in my favour, and the stream was fast and tortuous with banks, eddies, and innumerable islands and cross channels, so that the navigation occupied all one's energy,

---

* Knapsack, from "schnap," "sach," provision bag, for "bits and bats," as we should say; havresack is from "hafer," "forage bag." Query.—Does this youthful carriage of the knapsack adapt boys for military service, and does it account for the high shoulders of many Germans?

† In the newspaper accounts of the weather it was stated that at this time a storm swept over Central Europe.

especially as it was a point of honour not to haul down the sail in a fair wind.

Midday came, and yet I could find no place to breakfast, though the excitement and exertion of thus sailing was really hard work. But still I hurried on, for dark clouds were gathering behind, and thunder and rain seemed very near.

"Ah," said I inwardly, "had I only listened to that worthy dame's entreaties this morning that I should take good provision for the day!" She had smiled like the best of mothers all the time I took coffee, and timidly asked to be allowed to touch my watch-chain, "it was so *schön*," so beautiful to see. But, oddly enough, I had taken no solid food on board to-day, being so impatient to get off when the wind was strong and fair. The rapid pace then brought us to Ehingen, the village I had marked on the map for this night's rest. But now I got there I found out it was *too soon*—I could not stop for the day with such a splendid breeze inviting progress; nor would it do to leave the boat on the bank and go to the village to eat, for it was too far, and so I just let the current and sails hurry us on as before.

Now and then I asked some gazing agriculturist on the bank where the nearest houses were, but he never could understand that I meant *nearest, and also close to the river;* so the end of every discussion was that he said, "Ya vol," which means in Yankee tongue, "That's so"; in Scottish, "Hoot, aye"; in Irish, "Troth, an' it is"; and in French, "C'est vrai"; but then none of this helps one a bit.

I therefore got first ravenous and then faint, and after mounting the bank to see the turns of the river in advance, I actually fell asleep under a tree. The wind had quite subsided when I awoke, and I quaffed deep draughts of water and paddled on. The banks were now of mud, and about eight or ten feet high, quite straight up from the water, just like those on the Nile, and several affluent streams ran from the plain to join the river. Often, indeed, I saw a church tower right ahead, and laboured along to get there, but after half-a-mile the stream would turn sharp round to one side, and still more and more round, and at last the tower once in front was directly behind us. The explanation of this tormenting peculiarity was simply this,—that the villages were carefully built *away* from the river bank because it is a bad foundation, and is washed away as new channels are formed by the flood.

When the light began to fail I took a good look at the map, and serpentine bends were given there plain enough indeed, but only in one-half of their actual number; and, moreover, I saw that in the forest we had now entered I must expect no suitable villages at all. The overhanging trees made a short twilight soon deepen into night; and to add to the interest the snags suddenly became numerous, and some of them waved about in the current, as they do on the Upper Mississippi, when the tenacious mud holds down the roots merely by its weight. All this made it necessary to paddle slowly and with great caution, and to cross always to the slack side of the stream instead of by one's usual course, which, in descending, is to keep with the rapid current.

Sometimes I had to back out of shallows which were invisible in the dark, and often I stopped a long time before a glance of some ripple obscurely told me the probable course. The necessity for this caution will be evident when it is remembered that in case of an upset here both sets of clothes would have been wet together, and without any house at hand to dry them.

All at once I heard a bell toll quite near me in the thick wood, and I came to the bank, but it was impossible to get ashore on it, so I passed that place, too, and finally made up my mind to sleep in the boat, and had all sorts of plans in course of devising.

Just then two drops of rain came on my face, and I resolved at once to stop, for if my clothes got wet before I was snug in the canoe there would be little comfort all night, without anything solid to eat since morning, and all my cigars already puffed away.

As I was cautiously searching for a root projecting from the bank to make fast to, a light appeared straight in front, and I dashed forward with the boat to reach it, and speedily ran her into a strange sort of lake or pond, where the stream ceased, and a noise on the boat's side told of weeds, which proved to be large round leaves on the surface, like those of the Victoria Regia lily.

I drew up the boat on shore, and mounted the high bank through a thicket, carrying my long paddle as a protection against the large dogs which farmhouses sport here, and which might be troublesome to quarrel with in the dark. The house I came to on the top of the precipice had its window lighted, and several people were talking inside, so I knocked loudly, and all was silence. Then I knocked again, and whined out that I was a poor benighted "Englander," and hoped they would let me in, at which melancholy tale they burst out laughing, and so did I! After an argument between us, which was equally intelligible on both sides, a fat farmer cautiously took the light upstairs, and, opening a window, thrust the candle forward, and gazed out upon me standing erect as a true Briton, and with my paddle, too, but in reality a humiliated vagrant begging for a night's lodging.

After due scrutiny he

pulled in his head and his candle, shut the window, and fell to laughing immoderately. At this I was glad, for I never found it difficult to get on with a man who begins in good humour.

Presently the others went up, and I stood their gaze unflinchingly, and, besides, made an eloquent appeal in the vernacular (mine, not theirs, be it clearly understood). They were satisfied that I was alone, and, though probably mad, yet not quite a match for all of them, so they came down gallantly; but then there was the difficulty of persuading the man to come to the river on this dark night to carry up a boat.

With some exertion we got it up by a better way, and safely locked it in the cowhouse of another establishment, and then I was made thoroughly comfortable. They said they had nothing to eat but kirchwasser, bread, and eggs, and how many eggs would I like? so I said, "To begin with, ten," and I ate them every one. By this time the priest had come. They often used to send for the prester to do the talk; and the large room soon got full, and the sketch-book was passed round, and an India-rubber band made endless merriment for the smaller fry, all in the old routine, the very mention of which it may be tedious to hear of so often, as indeed it was to me to perform.

But then in each case it was *their* first time of going through the performance, and they were so kind and courteous one could not refuse to please such people. The priest was very communicative, and we tried to converse in Latin, for my German was not good enough for him nor his French for me. But we soon agreed that it was a long time since our schoolboy Latin days, though I recollect having had long conversations in Latin with a monk at Nazareth, but there we had ten days together, and so had time to practise.

Thus ended the 1st of September, the only occasion on which I had to " rough it" at all during the voyage; and even then, it may be seen, the very small discomforts were all the results of gross want of prudence on my own part, and ended merely by a hard day's work with breakfast and dinner merged into a late supper. My bill here was 3s. 6d., the day before, 4s. 6d., including always wine and luxuries.

CHAPTER VI.

Day-dream—River Iller—Ulm—A stiff king—Lake Constance—Seeing in the dark—Coloured Canvas—Sign talk—Synagogue—Amelia.

THE threatening rain had not come during the night, and it was a lovely morning next day, like all the rest before and after it; and as I was leaving this place I found it was called Gegglingen, and was only nine miles from Ulm.

The lofty tower of the Cathedral of this town soon came in view, but I noticed it without any pleasure, for this was to end my week on the Danube; and in my ship's log I see it is entered as "one of the most pleasant weeks of my life for scenery, health, weather, exercise, and varied adventure."

In a pensive mood, therefore, I landed at a garden, and reclined to have a rest and a daydream, but very soon the loud booming of artillery aroused the hill echoes, and then sharp rattling of infantry firing. The heights around were crested with fringes of blue-coated soldiers and glistening bayonets, amid the soft, round, cotton-like volumes of smoke from the great guns spurting out fire long before the sound comes. It was a review of troops and a sham attack on a fort surmounting the hill, near the battlefield of long years ago at Ulm. If they fought in heat and fury, let them now rest in peace.

Come back, my thoughts, to the river at my feet.

I had been with this river from its infancy, nay, even from its birth in the Schwartzwald. I had followed it right and left, as it seemed to toddle in zigzag turnings like a child; and I had wound with it hither and thither as it roamed away farther like free boyhood. Then it grew in size by feeding on the oozy plain, and was still my companion when it got the strength of youth, dashing over the rocks, and bounding among the trees; and I had come at last to feel its powerful stream stronger than my strength, and compelling my respect. And now, at Ulm, I found it a noble river, steady and swift, as if in the flower of age; but its romance was gone. It had boats on it, and navigation, and bridges, and railways, like other great waters; and so I would let it go on alone, tumbling, rushing, swelling, till its broad bosom bears whole fleets at Ofen, and at length as a great water giant it leaps down headlong into the Black Sea.

Having seen Ulm in a former tour, I was in no mood to "go over" the sights again, nor need they be related here, for it is only river travel and lake sailing that we are concerned with; while reference may be made to the Guide-books if you wish to hear this sort of thing: "Ulm, lat. 97°, an old Cathedral (*a*) town, on two (§) hills (see Appx.). Pop. 20,001; situated ✝✝ on the Danube." At that I stop, and look into the water once more.

The river is discoloured here,—what is called in Scotland "drumly;" and this seems partly owing to the tributary *Iller*, which rises in the Tyrol, and falls into the Danube, a little way above the town. The Iller has a peculiar air of wild, forlorn bleakness, with its wide channel half occupied by cold white gravel, and its banks scored and torn, with weird, broken roots, gnarled trees, barkless and fallen, all lying dishevelled; surely in flood times, and of dark wintry nights, a very deluge boils and seethes along there.

Then, at last, there are the barges on the Danube, and very rudimental they are. Huge in size, with flat bottoms, and bows and stems cocked up, and a roofed house in the middle of their sprawling length. The German boys must have these models before them when they make the Noah's Arks for English nurseries; and

Murray well says of these barges, they are "nothing better than wooden **sheds** floating in flat trays."

In 1839 a steamer was tried here, but it got on a bank, and the effort was abandoned; so you have to go on to Donauwerth before this mode of travelling is reached, but from thence you can **steam** down to the Black Sea, and the passage-**boats below** Vienna are very fast and well **appointed**.

Rafts there are at Ulm, but I suppose the timber for them comes by the Iller, for I did not notice any logs descending the upper part of the Danube.

Again, there are the public washhouses in the river, each of them a large floating establishment, with overhanging eaves, under which there are, say, fifty women all in a **row,** half kneeling or leaning over the low bulwarks, and all slapping your best shirts mercilessly.

I made straight over to these ladies, **and** asked how the Rob Roy could get up so steep a bank, **and** how far it was to the railway; and so their senior matron kindly got a man and a hand-cart for the boat, and, as the company of women heard it was from England, they all talked louder **and** more together, **and** pounded and smacked the unfortunate linen with additional emphasis.

The bustle at the railway-station was only half about the canoe; the other half was for the King of Wurtemburg, who was getting into his special train to go to his palace at Fredrickshafen.

Behold me, then, fresh from Gegglingen and snags, in the immediate presence of Royalty! But this King was not at all kingly, though decidedly stiff. He is, however, rather amusing sometimes; as when by his order, issued lately, he compels sentries to salute even empty Royal carriages.

I got a newspaper here, and had twelve days to overtake of the world's doings while I had been in hill, forest, and waves. Yet I had been always asked there to "give the news," and chiefly on two points,—the Great Eastern, with its electric cable, and the catastrophe on the Matterhorn glacier, the two being at times vaguely associated, as if the breaking of the cable in the one had something to do with the loss of mountaineers in the other.

So, while I read, the train bore us southwards to Fredrickshafen, the canoe being charged as baggage three shillings, and patiently submitting to have a numbered label pasted on its pretty brown face.

Fredrickshafen, on the north side of the Lake of Constance, has a charming view in front of it well worth stopping to enjoy. It is not fair to treat it only as a half-hour's town, to be seen while you are waiting for the lake steamer to take you across to Switzerland.

But now I come to it for a Sunday's rest (if **you wish to travel fast** and far, rest **every Sunday), and, as the hotel** faced the station, **and the lake faced** the hotel, this is the very place to stop in with a canoe.

So I took the boat upstairs into a loft, where the washerwoman of the hotel not only gave room for the well worked timbers of the Rob Roy to be safe and still, but kindly mended my sails, and sundry other odds and ends of a bachelor's wardrobe, somewhat disorganized **by** rough times.

Next day there was service in the Protestant church, a fine building, well filled, **and** duly guarded by a beadle in bright array.

The service began by a woman singing "Comfort ye" from Handel, in exquisite and simple style, with a voice that made one forget how this solemn melody is usually sung by a man. Then a large number of school children were ranged in the chancel, round a crucifix, and sang a very beautiful hymn, and **next the** whole **congre-**

gation joined in chanting the psalms in unison, with tasteful feeling and devoutness. A young German preacher gave us an eloquent sermon, and then the people were dismissed.

The afternoon was drummed away by **two noisy bands,** evidently rivals, and each determined to excel the other in loudness, while both combined to persecute the **poor** visitors who *do* wish **for** quietness, at any **rate** once a week. I could scarcely escape from this din in a long walk by the lake, and **on** coming back found a man bathing by moonlight, while rockets, squibs, and Catherine wheels were let off in his boat. Better by far was it **to look with** entranced eyes on the far off snowy range, now lit up by the full harvest moon, and on the sheen of "each particular star," bright above, and bright again below, in the mirror of the lake.

The Lake of Constance is forty-four miles long, and about nine miles wide. I could not see a ripple there when the Rob Roy was launched at early morn, with my mind, and body, and soul refreshed, and an eager longing to begin the **tour of** Switzerland over again, but now in so new a fashion. Soon **I was** far from the shore, and in that middle distance of the lake where all sides seem equally near, and where the "other side" appears never **to** get any nearer as you go on. Here, in the middle, I rested for a while, and the sensation then was certainly new. Beauty was everywhere around, and there was full freedom to see it. There was no cut-and-dry route to be followed, no road, not even a track on the water, no hours, or times to constrain. I could go right or left by a stroke of the paddle, and I was utterly **my own** master of whither to steer, and where **to stop.**

The " pat-a-pat " of a steamer's wheels was the **only** sound, and that was very distant, and when the boat came near, the passengers cheered the canoe, and smiles of (was it not?) envy told of how pleasant and pretty she looked. After a little wavering in my plans, I settled it was best to go to the Swiss side, and, after coasting by the villages, I selected a little inn in a retired bay, and moored **my** boat, **and** ordered breakfast. Here was an old man of eighty-six, landlord and waiter in **one, a venerable** man, and I respect age more as I grow **older.** He talked with me for five hours while I ate, read, and sketched, and feasted my eyes on mountain views, and answered vaguely to his remarks, said in a sleepy way, and in a hot, quiet, basking sun. There are peaceful and almost dreamy hours of rest in this water tour, and they are sweet too after hard toil. It is not all rapids and struggles when **you** journey with a canoe.

Close to the inn was the idiot asylum, an old castle with poor demented women in it. The little flag of my boat attracted their attention, and all the inmates were allowed to come out and see it, with many smiles of pleasure, and many odd remarks and gestures.

Disentangling myself from this strange group, I landed again further down, and, under a splendid tree, spent an hour or two in carpenter's work (for I had a few tools on board), to repair the boat's damages and to brighten her up a bit for the English eyes I must expect in the next part of the voyage.

Not a wave had energy to rise on the lake in the hot sun. A sheep-bell tingled now and then, but in a tired, listless, and irregular way. A gossamer spider had spun his web from my mast to the tree above, and wagtails hopped near me on the stones, and turned an inquiring little eye to the boat and its master reclining on the grass. It was an easy paddle from this to the town of Constance, which is at the end of the lake.

Here a *douanier* made a descent upon me and was inexorable. "You *must* have the boat examined." "Very well, pray examine it." The officer was absent, and I must put the canoe in the Custom-house till to-morrow morning. An hour was wasted in palaver about this, and at first I protested vigorously against such absurdity in "free Switzerland." But Constance is not in Switzerland, it is in the Grand Duchy of Baden, and so to keep it "grand," they must do very little things, and at any rate can trouble travellers. At length an obliging native, ashamed of the proceeding, remonstrated with the douanier, and persuaded him at least to search the boat and let it pass.

He took as much time to do this as if it were a bark of 300 tons, and, when he came to look at the stern, I gravely pointed to a round hole cut in the partition for this very purpose! Into this hole he peered, while the crowd was hushed in silence, and as he saw nothing but darkness, extremely dark (for nothing else was there), he solemnly pronounced the canoe "free," and she was duly borne to the hotel.

But Constance once had a man in it who was really "grand," John Huss, the noble martyr for the truth. In the Council Hall you see the veritable cell in which he was imprisoned some hundreds of years ago, and on a former visit I had seen, from the tower, through a telescope, the field where the faggots burned him, and from whence his great soul leaped up to heaven out of the blazing pile.

Does not a thought or two on such great things make other common things look small?

True and good—but we may not stop always in the lake to ponder thus, for the current is moving again, so let us launch the Rob Roy on our old friend, the Rhine.

It is a change to cross a quiet lake after being hurried on a rapid stream like the Danube, and now it is another change to paddle from the lake into a wide river like the Rhine, which speeds fast and steady among lively scenes. The water is deep, and of a faint blue, but clear enough to show what is below. The pebbly bottom seems to roll towards you from underneath, and village churches appear to spin quietly round on the banks, for the land and its things seem to move, not the water, so glassy its surface steadily flowing.

Here are the fishers again, slowly paying out their fine-spun nets, and there is a target-hut built on four piles in the river.

The target itself is a great cube of wood, say six feet on each side. It is fired at from another hut perched also on posts in the water, and a marker safely placed behind the great block of wood turns it round on a vertical pivot, and so patches up the bullet-hole, and indicates its position to those who have fired.

The Rhine suddenly narrows soon after leaving

the Boden See, or Lake Constance as we call it, but the banks again open out till it is a mile or two in breadth. Here and there are grassy islands, and you may notice, by long stakes stuck on the shallows, which tremble as the water presses them, that the channel for steamers is very roundabout, though the canoe may skim over any part of it comfortably. Behind each islet of tall reeds there is a fishing-boat held fast by two poles stuck in the bottom of the river; or it is noiselessly moving to a more lucky pool, sculled by the boatman, with his oar at only one side,—rather a novel plan,—while he pays out the net with his other hand. Rudely-made barges are afloat, and seem to turn round helplessly in the current of the deeper parts, or hoist their great square sails in the dead calm—perhaps for the appearance of the thing—a very picturesque appearance, as the sail has two broad bands of dark blue cloth for its centre stripes. But the pointed lateen sail of Geneva is certainly a more graceful rig than the lug, especially when there are two masts, and the white sails swell towards you, goosewinged, before a flowing breeze.

The river has probably a very uneven bottom in this part, for the water sometimes rushes round in great whirlpools, and strange overturnings of itself, as if it were boiling from below in exuberant volume with a gushing upwards; and then again, it wheels about in a circle with a sweep far round, before it settles to go onward.*

On the borders of Switzerland the German and French tongues are both generally known at the hotels, and by the people accustomed to do business with foreigners travelling among them.

But in your course along a river these convenient waiters and polyglot commissionaires are not found exactly in attendance at every village, and it is, therefore, to the bystanders or casual loungers your observations must be addressed.

Frequent intercourse with natives of strange countries, where there is no common language **between** them and the tourist, will gradually teach him a "sign language" which suits all people alike.

Thus, in any place, no matter what was their

---

* These maelstroms seem at first to demand **extra** caution **as you** approach, **but** they are harmless enough, for the water is deep, and it **only** twists the boat round; and you need not mind this except when the sail is up, but have a care *then* **that you** are **not taken aback.** In crossing one of these whirlpools at full speed it will be found needless **to** try **to counteract** the sudden action on your bow by paddling **against** it, for it is better to hold on as if there were no interference, and presently the action in the reverse direction puts all quite **straight.**

dialect, it was always easy to induce one or two men to aid in carrying the canoe. The *formula* for this was something in the following style.

I first got the boat on shore, and a crowd of course soon collected, while I arranged its interior, and sponged out the splashed water, and fastened the cover down. Then, tightening my belt for a walk, I looked round with a kind smile, and selecting a likely man, I would address him in English deliberately as follows—suiting each action to the word, for I have always found that sign language is made more natural when you speak your own tongue all the time you are acting:—"Well now, I think as you have looked on enough and have seen all you want, it's about time to go to an hotel, a *gasthaus*. Here! you—yes, *you!*—just take that end of the boat up, so,—gently, 'langsam!' 'langsam!'"— all right, yes, under your arm, like this,—now march off to the best hotel, *gasthaus*."

Then the procession naturally formed itself. The most humorous boys of course took precedence, because of services willing to be performed; and, meanwhile, they gratuitously danced about and under the canoe like the Fauns around Silenus. Women only came near and waited modestly till the throng had passed. The seniors of the place kept on the safer confines

"Usual Procession."

of the movement, where dignity of gait might comport with close observation.

In every case of sign talking like the foregoing we have been helped by one substantive and one adverb; and if you pronounce these clearly, and use them correctly, while all the other expressions are evidently *your* language and not theirs, they will understand it much better than if you say the whole in bad German, and so give rise to all possible mistakes of your meaning.

But it is quite another matter when you have forgotten (or have never acquired) the foreign word for the noun you wish to name, though, even then, by well chosen signs, and among an intelligent people, a good deal can be conveyed, as may be shown in the following cases.

Once I was riding among the Arabs along the Algerian coast, on my way from Carthage, and my guide, a dense Kabyle, was evidently taking me past a place I wished to visit, and which had been duly entered in his list when I engaged him.

I could not make him understand this, for my limited Arabic had been acquired under a different pronunciation in Syria; but one night, it happened that a clever chief had me in a tent, or rather a hut, just like the top of a gipsy cart. I explained to him by signs (and talking English) that I was being led past what I wished to see. Then I tried to pronounce the name of that place, but was always wrong, or he could not make it out; it was Maskutayn, or "bewitched waters," a wonderful volcanic valley, full of boiling streams and little volcanoes of salt.

At length, sitting in the moonlight, I tried signs even for this difficult occasion. I put my chibouque (pipe) under the sand and took water in my hand, and as he looked on intently (for the Arabs love this speaking action) I put water on the fire in the pipe-bowl, and blew it up through the sand, talking English all the time. This I did again, and suddenly the black lustrous eyes of the Ishmaelite glistened brighter. He slapped his forehead. He jumped up. I could almost be sure he said "I know it now;" and then he roused the unfortunate muleteer from his snorings to give him an energetic lecture, by means of which I was directed next day straight (but in another direction) to the very place I desired to find.

In a few cases of this international talking it becomes necessary to sketch figures, which are even better than signs, but not among Arabs. During a visit to the fair of Nijni Novgorod, in the middle of Russia, I passed many hours in the "Chinese street" there, and found it was very difficult to communicate what I wished to say, and even signs were useless. But they had some red chalk or wax about the tea-chests, and there was a white wall beside us, and on it I put the whole story in large pictures, with an explanatory lecture in English all the time, which proceeding attracted an audience of several scores of Chinamen and Kalmuks and other outlandish people, and the particular group I meant to enlighten seemed perfectly to understand all that was desired.

And so I suppose that if you can work your paddle well, and learn the general sign language, and a little of the pencil tongue, you can go very far in a canoe without being starved or homeless; while you are sure to have a wide field in which to study the various degrees of intelligence among those you deal with.

To come back, however, from the **Volga to the Rhine.**

The current **flows more and more** gently as we enter the **Zeller See**, or Unter See, a lake which **would be called pretty if** one had not been spoiled **for a while by having a** snowy range **for** the background to the views on Constance.

But the Lake of Constance sadly wants islands, and here in the Zeller See are several, one of them being of great size. The Emperor of the French had passed two days at his chateau on this lake, just before **I arrived.** No doubt he would have waited a week had he known the Rob Roy **was** coming.

However, **as we were too** late to breakfast with his Majesty, I pulled in at the village **of** Steckborn, where an inn is built on **the actual** edge of the water, a state of things most convenient for the aquatic tourist, and which you find often along this part of the Rhine. For in a case of this sort you can tap at the door with the paddle, and order a repast before you debark, so that it is boiling and fizzing, and the table is all ready, while you put things to rights on board, and come leisurely ashore, and then tie the boat to the window balcony, or, at any rate, in some place where it can be seen all the time you breakfast or dine, and rest, and read, and draw.

Experience proved that very few boys, even of the most mischievous species, will meddle with a boat which is floating, but that very few men, even of the most amiable order, will refrain from pulling it about when the little craft is left on shore.

To have your boat not only moored afloat but in your sight too, that is perfection, and it is worth additional trouble to arrange this, because then, and for hours of the midday stoppage, you will be wholly at ease, or, to say the least, you will have one care the less. The weary resting traveller will not then be anxious about his absent boat, as if it were a valuable horse in a strange stable.

The landlord was much interested in the story of my voyage as depicted in the sketch-book, so he brought a friend to see me who could speak French, and who had himself constructed a boat of two tin tubes, on which a stage or frame is supported, with a seat and rowlocks, the oddest looking thing in nautical existence. I persuaded him to put this institution into the water, and we started for a cruise; the double-tube metal boat, with its spider-like gear aloft, and the oak canoe, so low and rakish, with its varnished cedar deck, and jaunty flag, now racing side by side, each of them a rare sight, but the two together quite unprecedented.

The river here is like parts of the Clyde and the Kyles of Bute, with French villages let in, and an Italian sky stretched overhead. We rowed across to a village where a number of Jews live, for I wished to visit their Synagogue; but, lo! this was the Grand Duchy of Baden land, so a heavily-armed sentry found us invading the dominion, and he would force us to land somewhere else. The man was civil, but his orders were unreasonable, so we merely embarked again and went over to Switzerland, and ran our little fleet into a bramble bush, to hide it while we mounted to an auberge on the hill and had a sixpenny bottle of wine.

The pretty Swiss lass in charge said she once knew an Englishman—"it was a pity they were all so proud." He had sent her a letter in English, which I asked her to let me read for her. It began, "My dear little girl, I love you;" and this did not sound so very proud for a beginning. My boating friend promised to make her a tin *cafetiere*, and I thus divined that he was the tinman of the village, and a most agreeable tinman too.

She came to see us on board, and her father arrived just in time to witness a triangular parting, which must have puzzled him a good deal, Amelia waving farewell to a " proud " Englishman and a nautical whitesmith, who both took leave also of each other, the last sailing away with huge square yards and coloured canvas, and the Rob Roy drifting with the stream in the opposite direction.

Every day for weeks past had been as a picnic to me, but I prolonged this one into night, the air was so balmy and the red sun setting was so soon replaced by the white moon rising, and besides, the navigation here had no dangers, and there were villages every few miles.

When I had enough of it, cruising here and there by moonlight, I drew up to the town of Stein, but all was now lonely by the water-side. This is to be expected when you arrive late; however, a slap or two on the water with the paddle, and a loud verse of a song, Italian, Dutch, a pibroch, any noise in fact, soon draws the idlers to you, and it is precisely the idlers you want.

One of them readily helped me with the boat to an inn, where an excellent landlady greeted the strange guest. From this moment all was bustle there, and very much it was increased by a German guest, who insisted on talking to me in English, which I am sure I did not understand a bit better than the Germans who came to listen and look on.

CHAPTER VII.

Fog — Fancy pictures — Boy soldiers — Boat's billet — Eating — Lake Zurich — Lake Zug — Swiss shots — Fishing Britons — Talk-book.

IN the morning there was a most curious change of air; all around was in a dense white fog. Truly it was now to be "sensation rowing;" so I hastened to get off into this milky atmosphere. I have an idea that we passed under a bridge; at least the usual cheers sounded this time as if they were above me, but the mist was as thick as our best November Cheshire cheese fogs, and quite as interesting. On several occasions I positively could not see the bow of my boat, only a few feet from my nose. The whole arrangement was so unexpected and entirely novel, fast paddling on an invisible stream, that I had the liveliest emotions of pleasure without seeing anything at all.

But then fancy had free play all the time, and the pictures it drew were full of colour, and, after all, our impressions of external objects are only pictures, so say the philosophers; and why not then enjoy a tour in a fog, with a good album of pictures making the while in the brain?

Sounds too there were, but like those of witches and fairies—though I believe it was only the cackling of some antique washerwomen on the banks. However, I addressed the unseen company in both prose and poetry, and was full of emphasis, which now and again was increased by my boat running straight into the shore. The clearing away of the fog was one of the most interesting evolutions of nature to be seen. In one sort or other every traveller has enjoyed the quick or gradual tearing up of a fog curtain on mountain or moor, but here it was on a beauteous river.

I wish to describe this process, but I cannot. It was a series of " Turner pictures," with glimpses right and left, and far overhead, of trees, sky, castles, each lightened and shown for a moment, and then gauzed over again and completely hidden; while the mind had to imagine all the context of the scenery, and it was sure to be quite wrong when another gleam of sun disclosed what was there in reality. For it cleared away at last, and Father Sol avenged himself by an extra hot ray, for thus trifling with his beams.

The Rhine banks here were sloping but steep,

with pleasant meadows, vineyards, and woods, mingled with tolerable fairness to all three. In short, though I appreciate scenery with an eager admiration, any scenery did well when the genial exercise of the canoe was the medium for enjoying it.

Soon afterwards the woods thickened, the mountains rose behind them, the current got faster and faster, the houses, at first dotted on the knolls, got closer and more suburb like, and at last a grand sweep of the stream opened up Schaffhausen to the eye, while a sullen sound on the water warned of "rapids ahead." As I intended to keep them always in front, some caution was needed in steering, though there is no difficulty here, for steamboats navigate thus far, and of course it is easy for a canoe.

But when I glided down to the bridge there was the "Goldenen Schiff" hotel, and I resolved to patronise it on account of its name, and because there was a gigantic picture of a Briton on the adjoining wall. He was in full Highland costume, though the peculiar tartan of his kilt showed that there is a new clan we have not yet recognised.

Here began a novel kind of astonishment among the people; for when, on my arrival, they asked, "Where have you come from?" and were told, "From England," they could not understand how my course seemed as if in reality from Germany.

We had started early, and the short morning's work was soon over; and thus arriving early at Schaffhausen, there was all the day before me to wander about.

Drums and a band presently led me to **a corps of little** boys in full uniform, about 200 of them, **all with real** guns and with boy officers, most **martial to** behold, albeit they were munching apples between the words of command, and pulling wry faces at urchins of eight years old, who strove in vain to take long steps with short legs.

They had some skirmishing drill, and used small goats' horns to give the orders instead of bugles. These horns are **used** on the railways too, and the note is very clear, and may be heard well a long way off. Indeed I think much might be done in our own drill by something of **this** sort.

It is a short three miles to the Belle Vue, built above the falls of Schaffhausen, and in full view of this noble sight. These great falls of the Rhine looked much finer than I had recollected them some twelve years before; it is pleasant, but unusual, for one's second visit to such sights to be more striking than the first. At night they were splendidly illuminated by Bengal lights of different colours, and the effect of this on the tossing foam and rich full body of ever pouring water—or fire as it then seemed to be—was to present a spectacle of magical beauty and grandeur. To look at this I sat on the balcony of the hotel, and with many travellers from various lands around. On one side of me was a Russian, and a Brazilian on the other.

Next day, at the railway-station, I put the sharp bow of the Rob Roy in at the window of the "baggages" office, and asked for the "boat's ticket." The clerk did not seem at all surprised, for he knew I was an Englishman, and nothing is too odd, queer, mad in short, for Englishmen to do.

But the porters, guards, and engine-drivers made a good deal of talk before the canoe was safely stowed among the trunks in the van; and I now and then visited her there, just for company's sake, and to see that the sharp-cornered, iron-bound boxes of the American tourists had not broken holes in the oaken skin. I could not but survey, with some anxiety, the lumbering casks on the platform, waiting to be rolled in beside the canoe; and the fish baskets, iron bars, crates, and clumsy gear of all sorts, which at every stoppage is tumbled in or roughly shovelled out of the luggage-van of a train.

This care and sympathy for a mere boat may be called enthusiasm by those who have not felt the like towards inanimate objects linked to our pleasures or pains by hourly ties of interest; but others will understand how a friendship for the boat was felt more every day I journeyed with her: her strong points were better known as I tried them more, but the weak points, too, of the frail traveller became now more apparent, and the desire to bring her safely to England was rapidly increased when we had made the homeward turn. The mere cost of the railway ticket for the boat's carriage to Zurich was very trifling, about two or three shillings, and not so much as the expense of taking it between the stations and the hotels.

Submitting, then, to be borne again on wheels and through tunnels in the good old railway style, we soon arrive among the regular Swiss mountains, and where gather the Swiss tourists, for whom arise the Swiss hotels, those huge establishments founded and managed so as best to fatten on the wandering Englishman, and to give him homœopathic feeding while his purse is bled.

For suffer me again to have a little gossip about *eating*. Yes, it is a mundane subject, and undoubtedly physical; but when the traveller has to move his body and baggage along a route by his own muscles, by climbing or by rowing, or by whipping a mule, it is a matter of high moment, to him at least, that fibrine should be easily procurable.

If you wish, then, to live well in Switzerland and Germany go to German hotels, and avoid the grand barracks reared on every view-point for the English tourist. See how the omnibus, from the train or the steamer, pours down its victims into the landlords' arms. Papa and Mamma, and three daughters and a maid: well, of course *they* will be attended to. Here is another timid lady with an alpenstock, a long white cane people get when they arrive in Switzerland, and which they never know what on earth to do with. Next there will issue from the same vehicle a dozen newly-fledged Londoners; and the whole party, men and women, are so demure, so afraid of themselves, that the hotel-keeper does just what he likes with them, every one.

As a hapless bachelor, and without a courier, or heavy baggage, or young ladies, I enter too, and venture to order a cutlet and potatoes. After half-an-hour two chops come and spinach, each just one bite, and cold. I ask for fruit, and some pears are presented that grate on the knife, with a minute bunch of grapes, good ones I will acknowledge. For this I pay 2*s*.

Next day I row three miles down the lake, and order, just as before, a cutlet, potatoes, and fruit, but this time at a second-rate German inn. Presently appear two luscious veal cutlets, with splendid potatoes, and famous hot plates; and a fruit-basket teeming gracefully with large clusters of magnificent grapes, peaches, pears all gushing with juice, and mellow apples, and rosy plums. For this I pay 1s. 6d. The secret is that the Germans won't pay the prices which the English fear to grumble at, and won't put up with the articles the English fear to refuse.

Nor do I blame the hotel-keepers for their part in this business. They try to make as much money as they can, and everybody who is making money tries to do the same.

In the twilight the Rob Roy launched on the Lake of Zurich, so lovely by evening, cool and calm, with its pretty villages painted again on the water below, and soft voices singing, and slow music floating in the air, as the moon looked down, and the crests were silvered on far-off hills of snow.

I put up the little craft in a boathouse at a village where all seemed to be secure. It was the only time I had found a boathouse for my boat, and the only time when she was badly treated; for, next morning, though the man in charge appeared to be a solid, honest fellow, I saw at once that the canoe had been sadly tumbled about and filled with water, the seat cast off and floating outside, and the covering deranged and the sails untied, and the sacred paddle defiled by clumsy hands.

The man who suffered this to be perpetrated will not, I hope, forget the Anglo-German-French set-down he received (with a half-franc), and I shall not forget in future to observe the time-honoured practice of carrying the canoe invariably into the hotel.

Another piece of experience gained here was this, that to send your luggage on by a steamer, intending to regain it on your arrival, is far less of convenience than it is of anxiety and trouble, when you can readily take the baggage with you always and everywhere in your own boat.

For much of the charm of the next day's paddle on the lake consisted in its perfect independence of all previous arrangements, and in the absence of such thraldom as, " You must be here by ten o'clock;" or, "You have to sleep there at night." So now, let the wind blow as it likes. I could run before it, and breakfast at this village; or cross to that point to bathe; or row round that bay, and lunch on the other side of the lake, or anywhere else on the shore, or in the boat itself, as I pleased.

When quite sated with the water, I fixed on Horgen to stop at for a rest, to the intense delight of all the Horgen boys. How they did jump and caper about the canoe, and scream with the glee of young hearts stirred by a new sensation!

It was one of the great treats of this voyage to find it gave such hours of pleasure to the juvenile population in each place. Along the vista of my recollection as I think over the past days of this excursion, many thousand childish faces brimming with happiness range their chubby or not chubby cheeks.

These young friends were still more joyous when the boat was put into a cart, and the driver got up beside it, and the captain of the canoe began his hot walk behind.

A number of their mammas came out to smile on the performance, and some asked to have a passage to England in the boat, to which I had the stock reply, given day by day, "Not much room for the crinoline." Only once was there the rejoinder, that the lady would willingly leave her expansion at home; though on another occasion (and that in France, too) they answered, "We poor folks don't wear crinoline."

In every group there were various forms of inquisitiveness about the canoe. First, those who examined it without putting questions; and then those who questioned about it without examining. Some lifted it to feel the weight; others passed their hands along its smooth deck to feel the polished cedar; others looked underneath to see if there was a keel, or bent the rope to feel how flexible it was, or poised the paddle (when I let them), and said, "How light!" and then more critical inquirers measured its dimensions, tapped its sides with their knuckles, and looked wise; sketched its form, scrutinized its copper nails, or gently touched the silken flag, with its frayed hem and colour fading now; in all places this last item, as an object of interest, was always the first exclaimed about by the lady portion of the crowd.

It is with such little but pleasant trivialities that a traveller's day may be filled in this enchanting atmosphere where simply to exist, to breathe, to gaze, and to listen, are enough to pass the sunny hours, if not to engage the nobler powers of the mind.

The Lakes of Zurich and Zug are not far separate. About three hours of steady road walking takes you from one to the other, over a high neck of forest land, and a hot walk this was from twelve to three o'clock, in the brightest hours of the day. The heat and the dust made me eager again to be afloat. By the map, indeed, it seemed as if one could row part of this way on a river which runs into Zug, but maps are no guidance as to the fitness of streams for a boat. They make a black line wriggling about do for all rivers alike, and this tells you nothing as to the depth or force of the current, nor can the drivers or innkeepers tell much more, since they have no particular reason for observing how a river comports itself; their business is on the road.

The driver was proud of his unusual fare, a boat with an English flag, and he gave a short account of it to every friend he met, an account no doubt frightfully exaggerated, but always accepted as sufficient by the gratified listener. The worthy carter, however, was quite annoyed that I stopped him outside the town of Zug (paying thirteen francs for the cart), for I wished to get the canoe into the water unobserved, as the morning's work had left me yet no rest, and most sweet repose could best be had by floating in my boat. However, there was no evading the townspeoples' desire to see "the schiff in a cart from England." I took her behind a clump of stones, but they climbed upon the stones and stood. I sat down in a moody silence, but they sat down too in respectful patience. I tried then another plan, turned the canoe bottom upward, and began lining a seam of the planks with red putty. They looked on till it was done, and I began the same seam again, and told them all the others must be lined. This, at last, was too much for some of the wiser ones, who turned away and murmured about my slowness, but others at once took their places in the front row. It seemed unfriendly to go on thus any longer, and as it was cooler now, I pushed the boat into the lake, shipped my luggage on board, and after the usual English speech to them all, bid every one "adieu."*

New vigour came when once the paddle was grasped again, and the soft yielding water, and gentle heaving on its bosom had fresh pleasure now after the dusty road. It seems as if one must be spoiled for land travel by this smooth liquid journeying.

Zug is a little lake, and the mountains are over it only at one end, but then these are glorious hills, the Rigi and a hundred more, each behind another, or raising a peak in the gaps between. I must resolutely abstain from describing these here. The sight of them is well known to the traveller. The painted pictures of them in every

* This word, like other expressive French words, is commonly used in Germany and Switzerland.

shop window are faithful enough for those who have not been nearer, and words can tell very little of what is seen and felt when you fill the delighted eye by looking on the snowy range.

Near one end of the lake I visited the line of targets where the Switzers were popping away their little bullets at their short ranges, with all sorts of gimcrack instruments to aid them, lenses, crooks, and straps for the arms, hair-triggers, and everything done under cover too. Very skilful indeed are they in the use of these contrivances; but the weapons look like toy-guns after all, and are only one step removed from the crossbows you see in Belgium and France, where men meet to shoot at stuffed cockrobins fixed on a pole, and do not hit them, and then adjourn for beer.

The Swiss are good shots and brave men, and woe be to their invaders. Still, in this matter of rifle shooting their *dilettanti* practice through a window, at the short range of 200 yards, seems really childish when compared with that of the manly groups at Wimbledon, where, on the open heath, in sun or drifting hail, the burly Yorkshireman meets with the hardy Scot, and sends his heavier deadly bullet on a swift errand right away for a thousand yards in the storm.

Leaving the shooters to their bulls' eyes, I

paddled in front of the town to scan the hotels, and to judge of the best by appearances. Out came the boats of Zug to examine the floating stranger. They went round and round, in a criticising mood, just as local dogs strut slowly in circles about a new-come cur who is not known to their street, and besides is of ambiguous breed. These boats were all larger than mine, and most of them were brighter with plenty of paint, and universally they were encumbered with most awkward oars.

A courteous Frenchman in one of the boats told me all the Zug news in a breath, besides asking numerous questions, and giving a hasty commentary on the fishing in the lake. Finally, he pointed out the best hotel, and so the naval squadron advanced to the pier, led by the canoe. A gracious landlady here put my boat safe in the hotel coachhouse, and offered to give me the key of the padlock, to make sure. In the *salle à manger* were some English friends from London, so now I felt that here was an end of lone wanderings among foreigners, for the summer stream of tourists from England was encountered at this point.

An early start next morning found the mists on the mountains, but they were quickly furled up out of the way in festoons like muslin curtains.

We skirted the pretty villas on the verge of the lake, and hauled in by some apple-trees to rig up the sails. This could be done more easily when the boat was drawn ashore than when it was afloat; though, after practice, I found I could not only set the mast and hoist the sails "at sea," but could even stand up and change my coat, or tie the flag on the masthead, or survey a difficult channel, while the boat was rocking on the waves of a rapid.*

Sailing on a lake in Switzerland is a full reward for carrying your mast and sails unused for many a long mile. Sometimes, indeed, I wished I had not provided sails at all, but this was when they were not available. Every time they came into use again the satisfaction of having brought them was reassured.

In sailing while the wind is light you need not always sit, as must be done for paddling. Wafted by the breeze you can now recline, lie down, put your legs anyhow and anywhere, in the water if you like, and the peak of the sail is a shade between the sun and your eyes, while the ripples seem to tinkle cheerfully against the bow, and the

* This is so very useful in extending the horizon of view, and in enabling you to examine a whole ledge of sunken rocks at once, that it is well worth the trouble of a week or two's practice.

"Sailing on Lake Zug."

wavelets seethe by smoothly near the stern. When you are under sail the hill tops look higher than before, for now you see how far they are above your "lofty" masthead, and the black rocks on the shore look blacker when seen in contrast with a sail like cream.

After a cruise that left nothing more to see of

Zug, we put into port at Imyn, and though it is a little place, only a few houses, the boys there were as troublesome as gnats buzzing about; so the canoe had to be locked in the stable out of sight.

Three Britons were waiting here for the steamer. They had come to fish in Switzerland. Now fishing and travelling kill each other, so far as my experience goes, unless one of them is used as a *passetemps* because you cannot go on with the other. Thus I recollect once at the town of Vossevangen, in Norway, when we had to wait some hours for horses, it was capital fun to catch three trout with a pin for a hook fastened on the lash of a gig-whip.

The true fisherman fishes for the fishing, not for the fishes. He himself is pleased even if he catches nothing, though he is more pleased to bring back a full basket, for that will justify him to his friends.

Now when you stop your travelling that you may angle, if you catch nothing you grudge the day spent, and keep thinking how much you might have seen in it on the road. On the other hand, if you do happen to catch one or two fish, you don't like to leave the place where more might be taken, and your first ten miles after departure from it is a stage of reflection about pools, stones, bites, and rises, instead of what is going on all around. Worst of all, if you have hooked a fish and lost him, it is a sad confession of defeat to give up the sport then and resume the tour.

As for the three visitors at Imyn, they had just twenty minutes sure, so they breakfasted in five minutes, and in the next three minutes had got their rods ready, and were out in the garden casting as fast as possible, and flogging the water as if the fish also ought to be in a hurry to get taken. The hot sun blazed upon the bald head of one of these excited anglers, for he had not time to put on his hat. The other had got his line entangled in a bush, and of course was *hors de combat*. The third was a sort of light skirmisher, rushing about with advice, and pointing out shoals of minnows everywhere else but where his companions were engaged. However, they managed to capture a few monsters of the deep, that is to say, a couple of misguided gudgeons, probably dissipated members of their tribe, and late risers, who had missed their proper breakfasts. Ardent as I am with the rod I could not enjoy fishing after this sort.

To be in this tide of wandering Britons, and yet to look at them and listen to them as if you were distinct—this is a post full of interest and amusement; and if you can, even for one day, try to be (at least in thought) a Swiss resident or a Parisian, and so to regard the English around you from the point they are seen from by the foreigners whom they visit, the examination becomes far more curious. But this has been done by many clever tourists, who have written their notes with more or less humour, and with more rather than less severity; so I shall not attempt to analyse the strange atoms of the flood from our islands which overflows the Continent every year.

It is the fashion to decry three-fourths of this motley company as "snobs," "spendthrifts," or "greenhorns." With humble but firm voice I protest against this unfairness; nor can I help thinking that much of the hard criticism published by travellers against their fellows is a crooked way of saying, what it does not do to assert directly, that the writer has at any rate met some travellers inferior to himself.

Of course, among the Englishmen whom I met here and there in the course of this voyage there were some strange specimens, and their remarks were odd enough, when alluding to the canoe. One said, for example, "Don't you think it would have been more commodious to have had an attendant with you to look after your luggage and things?" The most obvious answer to this was probably that which I gave, "Not for me, if he was to be in the boat; and not for him, if he had to run on the bank."

And, again. Another Englishman asked in all seriousness about the canoe voyage, "Was it not a great waste of time?" And when I inquired how *he* had spent his vacation, he said, "Oh, I was all the time *at Brighton!*"

In returning once more to English conversation, one is reminded how very useless and unpractical are all the "Talk-books" published to facilitate the traveller's conversation in foreign languages. Whether they are meant to help you in French, German, Italian, or Spanish, these little books, with their well-known double columns of words and phrases, and their "Polite Letter-writer" at the end, all seem to be equally determined to force words upon you which you never will need to use; while the things you are always wanting to say in the new tongue are either carefully buried among colloquies on botany or precious stones, or among philosophical discussions about metaphysics, or else the desirable phrases are not in the book at all.

This need of a brief and good "Talk-book" struck me particularly when I had carefully marked in my German one all the pages which could never be required in the tour, so that I might cut them out as an unnecessary addition to the weight of my ship's library. Why, the little book, when thus expurgated, got so lamentably thin that the few pages left of it, as just possible to be useful, formed only a wretched skeleton of the original volume.

Another fault of these books is that half the matter in them is made up of what the imaginary chatting foreigner says to you, the unhappy Englishman, and this often in long phrases, or even in set speeches.

But when, in actual life, the real foreigner speaks to you, he somehow says quite a different set of words from any particular phrases you see in the book, and you cannot make out his meaning, because it does not correspond with anything you have learned.

It is evident that a dictionary is required to get at the English meaning of what is said to you by another; while a talk-book will suffice for what you wish to say to him; because you can select in it and compose from it before you utter any particular phrase.

The Danish phrase-book for Norway and Sweden is a tolerably good one, and it holds in a short compass all the traveller wants; but I think a book of this kind for each of the other principal languages might well be constructed on the following basis.

First, let us have the expression "I want," and then the English substantives most used in travel talk, arranged in alphabetical order, and with their foreign equivalents. Next, put the request "Will you," and after it place each of the verbs of action generally required by travellers. Then set forth the question, "Does the," with a column of events formed by a noun, verb, and preposition in each, such as "coach stop at," "road lead to," "steamer start from," &c.; and, lastly, give us the comprehensive "Is it," with a long alphabetical list of adjectives likely to be employed. Under these four heads, with two pages of adverbs and numerals, I think that the primary communications with a foreigner can be comprised; and as for conversations with him on special subjects, such as politics, or art, or scenery, these are practically not likely to be attempted unless you learn his language, and not merely some of its most necessary *words;* but this study of language is not the purpose for which you get a talk-book.

Having now delivered a homily on international talking, it is time to be on the move again.

CHAPTER VIII.

Sailing on Lucerne—Seeburg—River scenes—Night and snow—The Reuss—A dear dinner—Seeing a rope—Passing a fall—Bremgarten rapids.

WHEN the steamer at Imyn had embarked the three sportsmen, and the little pier was quiet, we got a cart out for the Rob Roy, and bargained to have it rumbled over the hill to the Lake of Lucerne for the sum of five francs—it is only half-an-hour's walk. The landlord himself came as driver, for he was fully interested about the canoe, and he did not omit to let people know his sentiments on the subject all along the way, even calling out to the men in the apple-trees, who had perhaps failed to notice the phenomenon which was passing on the road beneath them. There was a permanent joke on such occasions, and, oddly enough, it was used by the drivers in Germany as well as in Switzerland, and was of course original and spontaneous with each of them as they called out, "Going to America!" and then chuckled at the brilliant remark.

The village we came to on Lucerne was the

well-known Kussnacht, that is, *one* of the well-known Kussnachts, for there are plenty of these honeymoon towns in Central Europe; and with the customary assembly of *quidnuncs*, eloquently addressed this time by the landlord-driver, the canoe was launched on another lake, perhaps the prettiest lake in the world.

Like other people, and at other times, I had traversed this beautiful water of the Four Cantons, but those only who have seen it well by steamer and by walking, so as to know how it juts in and winds round in intricate geography, can imagine how much better you may follow and grasp its beauties by searching them out alone and in a canoe.

For thus I could penetrate all the wooded nooks, and dwell on each view-point, and visit the rocky islets, and wait long, longer—as long as I pleased before some lofty berg, while the ground-swell gently undulated, and the passing cloud shaded the hill with grey, and the red flag of a steamer fluttered in a distant sunbeam, and the plash of a barge's oar broke on the boatman's song; everything around changing just a little, and the stream of inward thought and admiration changing too as it flowed, but, all the time, and when the eye came back to it again, there was the grand mountain still the same,

"Like Teneriffe or Atlas unremoved."

How cool the snow looked up there aloft even in the heat of summer! and, to come down again to one's level on the water, how lively the steamer was with the music of its band and the quick beat of its wheels curling up white foam. Let us speed to meet it and to get a tossing in the swell, while **Jones and Smith**, under the awning, cry out, "Why, to be sure, that's the Rob Roy canoe," and Mrs. Jones and the three Miss Smiths all lift up their heads from their "**Murrays**," where they have been diligently reading the description in words of all the scenery around, although they have suffered its realities in mountain, wood, and lake to pass unnoticed.

As I was quite fresh (having worked chiefly the sails on Zug) and now in good "training," so as to get on very comfortably with ten or twelve hours' rowing in the day, I spent it all in seeing this inexhaustible Lake of Lucerne, and yet felt that at least a dozen new pictures had been left unseen in this rich volume of the book of nature.

But as this book had no page in it about quarters for the night it was time to think about these homely affairs, and to look out for an hotel; not one of the big barracks for Englishmen spoken of before, but some quiet place where one could stop for Sunday. Coming suddenly then round a shady point, behold the very place! But can it be an hotel? Yes, there is the name, "Seeburg." Is it quiet? Observe the shady walks. Bathing? Why, there is a bath in the lake at the end of the garden. Fishing? At least four rods are stretched over the reeds by hopeful hands, and with earnest heads behind, watching for the faintest nibble. Let us run boldly in. Ten minutes, and the boat is safely in a shed, and its captain well housed in an excellent room; and, having ordered dinner, it was delicious to jump into the lake for a swim, all hot with the long day's work, and to stretch away out to the deep, and circle round and round in these limpid waters, with a nice little bath-room to come back to, and fresh dry clothes to put on. In the evening we had very pretty English music, a family party improvised in an hour, and broken up for a moonlight walk, while, all this time (one fancied), in the big hotel of the town the guests were in stiff *coteries*, or each set retired to its sitting-room, and lamenting how unsociable everybody else had become.

I never was more comfortable than here, with a few English families "en pension," luxuriating for the sum of six francs per day, and an old Russian General, most warlike and courteous, who would chat with you by the hour, on the seat under the shady chestnut, and smiled at the four persevering fishermen whose bag consisted, I believe, of three bites, one of them allowed on all hands to have been *bonâ fide*.

Then on Sunday we went to Lucerne, to church, where a large congregation listened to a very good sermon from the well-known Secretary of the Society for Colonial and Continental Churches. At least every traveller, if not every home-stayed Englishman, ought to support this Association, because it many times supplies just that food and rest which the soul needs so much on a Sunday abroad, when the pleasures of foreign travel are apt to make only the mind and body constitute the man.

I determined to paddle from Lucerne by the river Reuss, which flows out of the lake and through the town. This river is one of four—the Rhine, Rhone, Reuss, and Ticino, which all rise near together in the neighbourhood of the St. Gothard; and yet, while one flows into the German ocean, another falls into the Mediterranean, both between them having first made nearly the compass of Switzerland.

The walking tourist comes often upon the rapid Reuss as it staggers and tumbles among the Swiss mountains. To me it had a special interest, for I once ascended the Galenhorn over the glaciers it starts from, and with only a useless guide, who lost his head and then lost his way, and then lost his temper and began to cry. We groped about in a fog until snow began to fall, and the snowstorm lasted for six hours—a weary time spent by us wandering in the dark and without food. At length we were discovered by some people sent out with lights to search for the benighted pleasure-seeker.

The Reuss has many cascades and torrent gorges as it runs among the rough crags, and it falls nearly 6,000 feet before it reaches the Lake of Lucerne, this lake itself being still 1,400 feet above the sea.

A gradual current towards the end of the lake entices you under the bridge where the river starts again on its course, at first gently enough, and as if it never could get fierce and hoarse-voiced when it has taken you miles away into the woods and can deal with you all alone.

The map showed the Reuss flowing into the Aar, but I could learn nothing more about either of these rivers except that an intelligent man said, "The Reuss is a mere torrent," while another recounted how a man some years ago went on the Aar in a boat, and was taken up by the police and punished for thus perilling his life.

Deducting from these statements the usual 50

per cent. for exaggeration, everything appeared satisfactory, so I yielded my boat to the current, and, at parting, waved my yellow paddle to certain fair friends who had honoured me with their countenance, and who were now assembled on the bridge. After this a few judicious strokes took the Rob Roy through the town and past the pleasant environs, and we were now again upon running water.

The current, after a quiet beginning, soon took a sort of "business air," as if it did not mean to dally, and rapidly got into quick time, threading a devious course among the woods, hayfields, and vineyards, and it seemed not to murmur (as streams always do), but to sing with buoyant exhilaration in the fresh brightness of the morn.

It certainly was a change, from the sluggish feeling of dead water in the lakes to the lively tremulous thrilling of a rapid river like the Reuss, which, in many places, is as wide as the Rhine at Schaffhausen. It is a wild stream, too fast for navigation, and therefore the villages are not built close to the water, and there are no boats, and the lonely, pathless, forest-covered banks are sometimes bleak enough when seen from the water.

For some miles it was easy travelling, the water being seldom less than two feet deep, and with rocks readily visible by the eddy bubbling about them, because they were sharp and jagged. It is the long smooth and round-topped rock which is most treacherous in a fast river, for the spray which the current throws round such a rock is often not different from an ordinary wave.

Now and then the stream was so swift that I was afraid of losing my straw hat, simply from the breeze created by great speed—for it was a day without wind.

It cannot be concealed that continuous physical enjoyment such as this tour presented is a dangerous luxury if it be not properly used. When I thought of the hospitals of London, of the herds of squalid poor in fœtid alleys, of the pale-faced ragged boys, and the vice, sadness, pain, and poverty we are sent to do battle with if we be Christian soldiers, I could not help asking, "Am I right in thus enjoying such comfort, such scenery, such health?" Certainly not right, unless to get vigour of thought and hand, and freshened energy of mind, and larger thankfulness and wider love, and so, with all the powers recruited, to enter the field again more eager and able to be useful.

In the more lonely parts of the Reuss the trees were in dense thickets to the water's edge, and the wild ducks fluttered out from them with a splash, and some larger birds like bustards often hovered over the canoe. I think among the flying companions I noticed also the bunting, or "ammer" (from which German word comes our English "yellow hammer"), wood-pigeons, and very beautiful hawks. The herons and kingfishers were here as well, but not so many of them as on the Danube.

Nothing particular occurred, although it was a pleasant morning's work, until I got through the bridge at Imyl, where an inn was high up on the bank. The ostler helped me to carry the boat into the stable, and the landlady audaciously charged me 4s. 6d. for my first dinner (I always had two dinners on full working days), being pretty sure, I dare say, that she need not expect her customer to stop there again.

The navigation after this began to be more interesting, with gravel banks and big stones to avoid, and a channel to be chosen from among several, and the wire ropes of the ferries stretched tightly across the river requiring to be noticed with proper respect.

It may be observed how difficult it is, sometimes, to see a rope when it is stretched and quite horizontal, or at any rate how hard it is to judge correctly of its distance from the spectator's eye. This can be well noticed in walking by the seashore among fishing-boats moored on the beach, when you will sometimes even knock against a taut hawser before you are aware that it is so close.

This is caused by the fact that the mind estimates the distance of an object partly by comparing the two views of its surface obtained by the two eyes respectively, and which views are not quite the same, but differ, just as the two pictures prepared for a stereoscope. Each eye sees a little round one side of the object, and its solid look and its distance are thus before the mind.

Now when the rope is horizontal the eyes do not see round the two sides in this manner, though if the head is leant sideways it will be found that the illusion referred to no longer appears.

Nor is it out of place to inquire thus at length into this matter, for I can assure you that one or two blunt slaps on the head from these ropes across a river make it interesting if not pleasant to examine "the reason why."

The actual number of miles in a day's work is much influenced by the number of waterfalls or artificial barriers which are too dry or too high to allow the canoe to float over them.

In all such cases, of course, I had to get out and to drag the boat round by the fields, as has been already described (p. 84); or to lower her

"SHIRKING A FALL." 155

"Shirking a Fall."

carefully among the rocks, as is shown in the accompanying sketch, which represents the usual appearance of this part of the day's proceedings. Although this sort of work was a change of posture, and brought into play new muscular action, yet the strain sometimes put on the limbs by the weight of the boat, and the great caution required where there was only slippery footing, made these barriers to be regarded on the whole as bores.

The river banks now suddenly assumed a new character. They were steep and high, and their height increased as we advanced between these two upright walls of stratified gravel and boulders.

A full body of water ran between them, the current being of only ordinary force at its edges, where it was interrupted by rocks, stones, and shingle, and was thus twisted into eddies innumerable.

To avoid these entanglements at the sides, it seemed best, on the whole, to keep the boat in mid-channel, though the breakers were far more dangerous there, in the full force of the stream.

I began to think that this must be the "hard place coming," which a wise man farther up the river had warned me was quite too much for so small a boat, unless in flood times, when fewer rocks would be in the way. In reply, I had told him that when I got near such a place I would pull out my boat and drag it along the bank, if requisite. To this he said, "Ah! but the banks are a hundred feet high." So I had mentally resolved (but entirely forgot) to stop in good time and to climb up the rocks and investigate matters ahead before going into an unknown run of broken water.

Such plans are very well in theory, but somehow the approach to these rapids was so gradual, and the mind was so much occupied in overcoming the particular difficulty of each moment, that no opportunity occurred for rest or reflection. The dull heavy roar round the corner got louder as the Rob Roy neared the great bend. For here the river makes a turn round the whole of a letter S, in fact very nearly in a complete figure of 8, and in wheeling thus it glides over a sloping ledge of flat rocks, spread obliquely athwart the stream for a hundred feet on either hand, and just a few inches below the surface.

The canoe was swept over this singular place by the current, its keel and sides grinding and bumping on the stones, and sliding on the soft moss which here made the rock so slippery and black.

The progress was aided by sundry pushes and jerks at proper times, but we advanced altogether in a clumsy, helpless style, until at length there came in sight the great white ridge of tossing foam where the din was great, and a sense of excitement and confusion filled the mind.

I was quite conscious that the sight before me was made to look worse because of the noise around, and by the feeling of the loneliness and powerlessness of a puny man struggling in a waste of breakers, where to strike a single one was sure to upset the boat.

From the nature of the place, too, it was evident that it would be difficult to save the canoe by swimming alongside it when capsized or foundered, and yet it was utterly impossible now to stop.

Right in front, and in the middle, I saw the well-known wave which is always raised when a main stream converges, as it rushes down a narrow neck. The depression or trough of this was about two feet below, and the crest four feet above the level, so the height of the wave was about six feet.

Though rather tall it was very thin and sharp-featured, and always stationary in position, though the water composing it was going at a tremendous pace. After this wave there was another smaller one, as frequently happens.

It was not the *height* of the wave that gave any concern; had it been at sea the boat would rise over any lofty billow, but here the wave stood still, and the canoe was to be impelled against it with all the force of a mighty stream, and so it *must* go through the body of water, for it could not have time to rise.

And so the question remained, "What is *behind* that wave?" for if it is a rock then this is the last hour of the Rob Roy.*

The boat plunged headlong into the shining mound of water as I clenched my teeth and clutched my paddle. I saw her sharp prow deeply buried, and then (I confess) my eyes were shut involuntarily, and before she could rise the mass of solid water struck me with a heavy blow full in the breast, closing round my neck as if cold hands gripped me, and quite taking away my breath.†

Vivid thoughts coursed through the brain in this exciting moment, but another slap from the lesser wave, and a whirl round in the eddy below, told that the battle was over soon, and the little boat slowly rose from under a load of water,

---

* I had not then acquired the knowledge of a valuable fact, that a sharp wave of this kind *never* has a rock behind it. A sharp wave requires free water at its rear, and it is therefore in the safest part of the river so far as concealed dangers are concerned. This at least was the conclusion come to after frequent observation afterwards of many such places.

† See a faithful representation of this incident, so far as relates to the water, in the Frontispiece.

which still covered my arms, and then, trembling, and as if stunned by the heavy shock, she staggered to the shore. The river too had done its worst, and it seemed now to draw off from hindering us, and so I clung to a rock to rest for some minutes, panting with a tired feeling of nervousness and gladness strangely mingled.

Although the weight of water had been so heavy on my body and legs, very little of it had got inside under the waterproof covering, for the whole affair was done in a few seconds, and though everything in front was completely drenched up to my necktie, the back of my coat was scarcely wet.

Most fortunately I had removed the flag from its usual place about an hour before, and thus it was preserved from being swept away.

Well, now it is over, and we are rested, and begin with a fresh start; but there is still some work to do in threading a way among the breakers. The main point, however, has been passed, and the difficulties after it look small, though at other times they might receive attention.

Here is our resting-place, the old Roman town of Bremgarten, which is built in a hollow of this very remarkable serpent bend of the rapid Reuss. The houses are stuck on the rocks, and abut on the river itself, and as the stream bore me past these I clung to the doorstep of a washerwoman's house, and pulled my boat out of the water into her very kitchen, to the great amusement and surprise of the worthy lady, who wondered still more when I hauled the canoe again through the other side of her room until it fairly came out to the street behind.

It must have astonished the people to see a canoe thus suddenly appearing on their quiet pavement. They soon crowded round and bore her to the hotel, which was a moderately bad one. Next morning the bill was twelve francs, nearly double its proper amount; and thus I had in one day the only two extortionate innkeepers met with at all.*

This quaint old place, with high walls and a foss, and several antiquities, was well worth the inspection of my early morning walk, and then the Rob Roy was ordered to the door.

* However, I made the landlord here take eight francs as a compromise.

CHAPTER IX.

Music at the mill—Sentiment and chops—River Limmat—Fixed on a fall—On the river Aar—Falls of Lauffenburg.—The cow cart.

The wetting and excitement of yesterday made me rather stiff in beginning again; and anon, when a rushing sound was heard in front I was aware of a little anxiety as to whether this might not mean the same sort of rough work as yesterday's over again, whereas hitherto this sound of breakers to come had always promised nothing but pleasure. However, things very soon came back to their old way, a continuous and varied enjoyment from morning to night.

The river was rapid again, but with no really difficult places. I saw one raft in course of preparation, though there were not many boats, for as the men there said, "How could we get boats *up* that stream?"

The villages near the river were often so high up on lofty cliffs, or otherwise unsuitable, that I went on for some miles trying in vain to fix on one for my (No. 1) dinner. Each bend of the winding water held out hopes that down there at last, or round that bluff cape at farthest, there must be a proper **place** to breakfast. But when it was now long past the usual **hour,** and the shores got less inhabited and hunger more **impe-**rative, I determined to land at a mill which overhung the stream in a very picturesque spot.

I landed unobserved. This was a blunder in **diplomacy, for** the canoe was always good as credentials; **but** I climbed up the bank and through the garden, and found the hall door open; so I walked timidly into a large, comfortable house, leaving my paddle outside lest it might be regarded as a bludgeon. I had come as a beggar, not a burglar.

The chords of a piano, well **struck and by firm** fingers, led me towards the drawing-room; **for** to hear music is almost to make sure of **welcome** in a house, and it was so now.

My bows and reverences scarcely **softened the** exceedingly strange appearance I must have made **as an** intruder, clothed **in** universal **flannel, and** offering ten thousand apologies in French, German, and English for thus dropping down from the clouds, that is to say, climbing up from the water.

The young miller rose from the piano, and

bowed. His fair sister stopped her sweet song, and blushed. For my part, I modestly asked for bread and wine, and got hopelessly involved in an effort to explain how I had come by the river unperceived. The excessive courtesy of my new friends was embarrassing, and was further complicated by the arrival of another young lady, even more surprised and hospitable.

Quickly the refreshments were set on the table, and the miller sealed the intimacy by lighting his ample pipe. Our conversation was of the most lively and unintelligible character, and soon lapsed into music, when Beethoven and Goss told all we had to say in chants and symphonies.

The inevitable sketch-book whiled away a good hour, till the ladies were joined by a third damsel, and the adventures of Ulysses had to be told to three Penelopes at once. The miller's party became humorous to a degree, and they resisted all my efforts to get away, even when the family dinner was set on the board, and the domestic servants and farm labourers came in to seat themselves at a lower table.

This was a picture of rural life not soon to be forgotten. The stately grandmamma of the mansion now advanced, prim and stiff, and with dignity and matronly grace entreated the stranger to join their company. The old oak furniture was lightened by a hundred little trifles worked by the women, or collected by the tasteful diligence of their brother; and the sun shone, and the mill went round, and the river rolled by, and all was kindness, "because you are an Englishman."

The power of the *Civis Romanus* is far better shown when it draws forth kindness, than when it compels fear. But it would not do to stop and eat, and it would not do to stop and not eat, or to make the potatoes get cold, or the granddames' dinner too late; so I *must* go, even though the girls had playfully hidden my luggage to keep the guest among them.

The whole party, therefore, adjourned to the little nook where I had left my boat concealed; and when they caught sight of its tiny form, and its little fluttering flag, the young ladies screamed with delight and surprise, clapping their hands and waving adieux as I paddled away.

I left this happy, pleasant scene with mingled feelings, and tried to think out what was the daily life in this sequestered mill; and if I got a little sentimental in my rowing, it may be pardoned by travellers who have come among kind friends where they expected perhaps a cold rebuff.

The romantic effect of all this was to make me desperately hungry, for be it known that bread and wine and Beethoven will not do to dine upon if you are rowing forty miles in the sun. So I must confess that when an hour afterwards I saw an auberge by the water's edge it became necessary to stifle my feelings by ordering an omelette and two chops.

The table was soon spread under a shady pear-tree just by the water, and the Rob Roy rested gently on the ripples at my feet.

The pleasures of this sunny hour of well-earned repose, freshened by a bunch of grapes and a pear plucked from above my head, were just a little troubled by a slight apprehension that some day the miller's sister might come by and hear how had been comforted my lacerated heart.

Again "to boat," and down by the shady trees, under the towering rocks, over the nimble rapids, and winding among orchards, vineyards, and wholesome scented hay, the same old story of constant varied pleasure. The hills were in front now, and their contour showed that some rivers were to join company with the Reuss, which here rolled on a fine broad stream, like the Thames at Putney.

Presently the Limmat flowed in at one side, and at the other the river Aar, which last then gives the name to all the three, though it did not appear to be the largest.

This is not the only Aar among the rivers, but it is the "old original Aar," which Swiss travellers regard as an acquaintance after they have seen it dash headlong over the rocks at Handek.

It takes its rise from two glaciers, one of them the Finster Aar glacier, not far from Grimsel; and to me this gave it a special interest, for I had been hard pushed once in the wilds near that homely Hospice.

It was on an afternoon some years ago, when I came from the Furca, by the Rhone glacier to the foot of the valley, walking with two Germans; and as they were rather "muffs," and meant to stop there, I thoughtlessly set off alone to climb the rocks and to get to the Grimsel by myself.

This is easy enough in daylight, but it was nearly six o'clock when I started, and late in September; so after a short half-hour of mounting, the snow began to fall, and the darkness was not made less by the white flakes drifting across it. By some wonderful conjuncture of things I managed to get over the mountain, but not by any path till I struck on a little stream which had often to be forded in the dark, but was always leading to the desired valley, until at length the welcome light of the Hospice was a haven to steer for, and I soon joined the pleasant English guests inside, and bought a pair of trousers from the waiter for 3s. 6d. for a change in the wet.

But paddling on the Aar had no great danger where I met it now, for the noisy, brawling torrent was sobered by age, and after much knocking about in the world it had settled into a steady and respectable river.

A few of my friends, the snags, were however lodged in the water hereabouts, and as they bobbed their heads in uneasy beds, and the river was much discoloured, it became worth while to keep a sharp lookout for them.

The "river tongue," explained already as consisting of sign language with a parallel comment in loud English, was put to a severe test on a wide stream like this. Consider, for example, how you could best ask the following question (speaking by signs and English only) from a man who is on the bank over there a hundred yards distant.

"Is it better for me to go over to those rocks, and keep on the left of that island, or to pull my boat out at these stumps, and drag her on land into this channel?"

One comfort is the man made out my meaning, for did he not answer, "Ya vol." He could not have done more had we both learned the same language, unless indeed he had *heard* what I said.

Mills occurred here and there. Some of these had the waterwheel simply built on the river; others had it so arranged as to allow the shaft to be raised or lowered to suit the varying height of water in floods and droughts. Others had it floating on barges. Others, again, had a half weir built diagonally across part of the river; and it was important to look carefully at this wall so as to see on which side it ought to be kept in selecting the best course. In a few cases there was another construction; two half weirs, converged gradually towards the middle of the river, forming a letter V, with its sharp end turned *up* the stream, and leaving a narrow opening there, through which a torrent flowed, with rough waves dancing merrily in the pool below.

I had to " shoot " several of these, and at other times to get out and lower the boat down them, in the manner explained before.

On one occasion I was in an unaccountably careless fit, and instead of first examining the depth of the water on the edge of the little fall, I resolved to go straight at it and take my chance.

It must be stated that while a depth of three inches is enough for the canoe to float in when all its length is in the water, the same depth will by no means suffice at the upper edge of a fall. For when the boat arrives there the fore part, say six or seven feet of it, projects for a time over the fall and out of the water, and is merely in the air, without support, so that the centre of the keel will sink at least six or seven inches; and if there be not more water than this the keel catches the crest of the weir, and the boat will then stop, and perhaps swing round, after which it must fall over sideways, unless considerable dexterity is used in the management.

Although a case of this sort had occurred to me before, I got again into the same predicament, which was made far more puzzling as the fore end of the boat went under a rock at the bottom of the fall, and thus the canoe hung upon the edge, and would go neither one way nor another. It would also have been very difficult to get out of the boat in this position, indeed it was not a feasible solution of the fix, and I fear the canoe was much wrenched in my struggles, which, however, ended by our tumbling down sideways, and, marvellous to say, quite safely to the bottom.

This performance was not one to be proud of.*

* This adventure was the result of temporary carelessness, while that at the rapids was the result of impatience, for the passage of these could probably have been effected

"Fixed on the fall."

Surely it was like ingratitude to treat the Rob Roy so, exposing it to needless risk when it had carried me so far and so well.

The Aar soon flows into the Rhine, and here is the Rob Roy on old Rhenus once more, with the town of Waldshut ("end of the forest") leaning over the high bank to welcome the canoe.

There is a lower path and a row of little houses without encountering the central wave had an hour or two been spent in examining the place. Let not any tourist, then, be deterred from a paddle on the Reuss, which is a perfectly suitable river, with no unavoidable dangers.

at the bottom of the cliff, past which the Rhine courses with rapid eddies deep and strong. Here an old fisherman soon spied me, and roared out his biography at the top of his voice; how he had been a courier in Lord Somebody's family; how he had journeyed seven years in Italy, and could fish with artificial flies, and was seventy years old, with various other reasons why I should put my boat into his house.

He was just the man for the moment; but first those two uniformed *douaniers* must be dealt with, and I had to satisfy their dignity by paddling up the strong current to their lair; for the fly had touched the spiders' web and the spiders were too grand to come out and seize it. Good humour, and smiles, and a little judicious irony as to the absurd notion of overhauling a canoe which could be carried on your back, soon made them release me, if only to uphold their own dignity, and I left the boat in the best drawing-room of the ex-courier, and ascended by stairs to the hotel aloft.

But the man came too, and he had found time to prepare an amended report of the boat's journey for the worthy landlord, so, as usual, there was soon everything ready for comfort and good cheer.

Waldshut is made up of one wide street almost

closed at the end, and with pretty gardens about it, and a fine prospect from its high position; but an hour's walk appeared to exhaust all the town could show, though the scenery round such a place is not to be done with in this brief manner.

The visitors soon came to hear and see more nearly what the newspapers had told them of the canoe. One gentleman, indeed, seemed to expect me to unfold the boat from my pocket, for a French paper had spoken about a man going over the country "with a canoe under his arm." The evening was enlivened by some magnesium wire signals, which I burned at the window of my bedroom to lighten up the whole street. This little entertainment was evidently—to the Waldshutians at least—entirely new.

Before we start homewards on the Rhine with our faces due West, it may be well very briefly to give the bearings and direction of the canoe's voyage up to this point.

First, by the Thames, E. (East), to Shoeburyness, thence to Sheerness, S. From that by rail to Dover, and by steamer to Ostend, and rail again to the Meuse, along which the course was nearly E., until its turn into Holland, N.E. Then to the Rhine, S.E., and ascending it nearly S., until at Frankfort we go N.E. by rail to

Asschaffenburg, and by the river wind back again to Frankfort in wide curves. Farther up the Rhine our course is due S., till from Freyburg the boat is carted E. to the Titisee, and to Donaueschingen, and descends the Danube, which there flows nearly E., but with great bends to N. and S. until we are at Ulm. The rail next carries us S. to the Lake of Constance, which is sailed along in a course S.W., and through the Zeller See to Schaffhausen, about due W. Thence turning S. to Zurich, and veering to the W. by Zug, we arrive on Lucerne, where the southernmost point of the voyage is reached, and then our prow points to N., till we land at Waldshut.

This devious course had taken the boat to several different kingdoms and states—Holland, Belgium, France, Wurtemburg, Bavaria, and the Grand Duchy of Baden, Rhenish Prussia, the Palatinate, Switzerland, and the pretty Hohenzollern Sigmaringen. Now we had come back again to the very Grand Duchy again, a land where all travellers must mind their p's and q's.

The ex-courier took the canoe from his wife's washing-tubs and put her on the Rhine, and then he spirited my start by recounting the lively parts I must expect soon to meet. I must take care to "keep to the right," near the falls of Lauffenburg, for an English lord had been carried over them and drowned;* and I must beware of Rheinfelden rapids, because an Englishman had tried to descend them in a boat with a fisherman, and their craft was capsized and the fisherman was drowned; and I must do this here, and that there, and so many other things everywhere else, that all the directions were jumbled up together. But it seemed to relieve the man to tell his tale, and doubtless he sat down to his breakfast comfortable in mind and body, and cut his meat into little bits, and then changed the fork to the right hand to eat them every one, as they all do hereabouts, with every appearance of content.

Up with the sails! for the East wind freshens, and the fair wide river hurries along. This was a splendid scene to sail in, with lofty banks of rock, and rich meads, or terraces laden with grapes. After a good morning's pleasure here the wind suddenly rose to a gale, and I took in my jib just in time, for a sort of minor hurricane came on, raising tall columns of dust on the road alongside, blowing off men's hats, and whisking up the hay and leaves and branches high into the air.

Still I kept the lug sail set; and with wind and

* This was Lord Montague, the last of his line, and on the same day his family mansion of Cowdray, in Sussex, was burned to the ground.

current in the same direction I scudded faster than I ever sailed before in my life. Great exertion was required to manage a light skiff safely with such a whirlwind above and a whirlwind below; one's nerves were kept in extreme tension, and it was a half-hour of pleasant excitement.

For this reason it was that I did not for some time notice a youth who had been running after the boat, yelling and shrieking, and waving his coat in the air. I drew nearer to him, and "luffed up," crying, "What's the matter?" and he could only pant out "Wasserfall, Wasserfall, funf minuten," so I found the breeze had brought me within a hundred yards of the falls of Lauffenburg.

I crossed to the right bank (as the ex-courier had directed), but the youth's loud cries to come to the "links," or left side, at last prevailed, and he was right in this. So I lowered the sail, and hauled the boat on a raft, and then this fine young fellow explained that five minutes more would turn the corner and get me into the horrid current sweeping over the falls.

I asked him to get a cart to convey the boat, and I had time to pull her up the high bank and make all snug for a drive, when he appeared again with a very grotesque carter and a most crazy vehicle, actually drawn by a milch cow!

All three of us laughed as we hoisted the Rob Roy on this cart, and the cow kicked vehemently, either at the cart, or the boat, or the laughing.

Our procession soon entered the little town, but it was difficult to be dignified. A cow drawing a boat to the door of a great hotel is certainly a quaint proceeding; although in justice to the worthy quadruped I should mention that she now behaved in a proper and lady-like manner. As the cart with a screeching wheel rattled slowly over the big round stones of the street, vacant at midday, the windows were soon full of heads, and after one peep at us, down they rushed to see the fun.*

Here the public hit upon every possible way but the right one to pronounce the boat's name, painted in blue letters on its bow. Sometimes it was "Roab Ro," at others "Rubree," but at length a man in spectacles called out, "Ah! ah! Valtarescote!" The mild Sir Walter's novels had not been written in vain.

The falls of Lauffenburg† can be seen well from the bridge which spans the river, much narrowed at this spot.

* A sketch of this cow-cart will be found, *post*, page 215.
† "Lauffenburg" means the "town of the falls," from "laufen," to run; and the Yankee term "loafer" may come from this, "herum laufer," one running about.

A raft was coming down at this very time—of course without the men upon it; and it was a very curious sight as the great solid frame seemed to resent the quickening of its solemn pace, and to hold back when every moment drew it nearer to the plunge.

Crash go all the bindings, and the huge, sturdy logs are hurled topsy-turvy into the gorge, bouncing about like chips of firewood, and rattling among the foam.

Nor was it easy to look calmly on this without thinking how the frail canoe would have fared in such a cauldron of cold water boiling.

The salmon drawn into this place get terribly puzzled by it, and so are caught by hundreds in great iron cages lowered from the rocks for this purpose.

Fishing stations of the same kind are found at several points on the river, where a stage is built on piles, and a beam supports a strong net below. In a little house, like a sentry box, you notice a man seated, silent and lonely, while he holds tenderly in his hand a dozen strings, which are fastened to the edges of the net. When a fish is beguiled into the snare, or is borne in by the swift current, the slightest vibrations of the net are thrilled along the cords to the watcher's hand, and he raises the great beam and secures the prize.

My young friend, who had so kindly warned me, and got the cow, and shown the salmon, I now invited to breakfast, and he became the hero of the hour, being repeatedly addressed by the other inquirers in an impossible German title, which signifies, in short, "Man preserver."

Here I heard again of a certain four-oared boat, with five Englishmen in it, which had been sent out from London overland to Schaffhausen, and then descended the Rhine rowing swiftly. This, the people said, had come to Lauffenburg about six weeks before, and I fully sympathized with the crew in their charming pull, especially if the weather was such as I had enjoyed; that is to say, not one shower in the boat from the source of the Danube to the Palace of Westminster.

CHAPTER X.

Field of Foam—Precipice—Puzzled—Rheinfelden Rapids—Dazzled—Astride—Very Salt—The Ladies—Whirlpool—Funny English—A baby—The bride.

THE canoe was now fixed on a hand-cart and dragged once more through the streets to a point below the falls, and the Rob Roy became very lively on the water after its few hours of rest. All was brilliant around, and deep underneath, and azure above, and happy within, till the dull distant sound of breakers got louder, and at last could not be ignored; it was the rapids of Rheinfelden.

The exaggeration with which judicious friends at each place describe the dangers to be encountered is so general in these latitudes, that one gets to receive it calmly, but the scene itself when I came to the place was certainly puzzling and grand.

Imagine some hundreds of acres all of water in white crested waves, varied only by black rocks resisting a struggling torrent, and a loud, thundering roar, mingled with a strange hissing, as

A FIELD OF FOAM.

the spray from ten thousand sharp-pointed billows is tossed into the air.

And then you are alone, too, and the banks are high, and you have a precious boat to guard.

While there was time to do it I stood up in my boat to survey, but it was a mere horizon of waves, and nothing could be learned from looking. Then I coasted towards one side where the shrubs and trees hanging in the water brushed the paddle, and seemed so safe because they were on shore.

The rapids of Bremgarten could probably be passed most easily by keeping to the edge, though with much delay and numerous "getting outs," but an attempt to go now along the side in this way was soon shown to be useless, for presently I came to a lofty rock jutting out into the stream, and the very loud roar behind it fortunately attracted so much attention that I pulled into the bank, made the boat fast, and mounted through the thicket to the top of the cliff.

I saw at once that to try to pass by this rock in any boat would be madness, for the swiftest part of the current ran right under the projecting crag, and then wheeled round and plunged over a height of some feet into a pool of foam, broken fragments, and powerful waves.

Next, would it be just possible to float the boat past the rock while I might hold the painter from above? The rock was found too high for this.

To see well over the cliff I had to lie down on my face, and the pleasant curiosity felt at first, as to how I should have to act, now gradually sickened into the sad conviction, "Impossible!" Then was the time to turn with earnest eyes to the wide expanse of the river, and see if haply, somewhere at least, even in the middle, a channel might be traced. Yes, there certainly was a channel, only one, very far out, and very difficult to hit upon when you sit in a boat quite near the level of the water; but the attempt must be made, or stay,—might I not get the boat carried round by land; under the trees far off were men who might be called to help, labourers quietly working, and never minding me. I was nearly tempted, but did not yield.

For a philosphical thought had come upmost, that, after all, I had not to meet *every* wave and rock now visible, and the thousand breakers dashing around, but only a certain few which would be on each side in my crooked and untrod way. Of the rocks in any one line—say fifty of them between me and any point—only two would become a near danger when I crossed that line. Then again, rapids look worse from the shore than they really are, because you see all their difficulties at once, and you hear the general din. On the other hand, waves look much smaller from the side (being half hidden by others) than you find them to be when the boat is in the trough between two. The hidden rocks may make a channel which looks good enough from the land, to be quite impracticable when you attempt it in the water.

Lastly, the current looks swifter from the shore where you observe its speed from a fixed point, than it does when looked at from the water where you notice only its velocity in relation to the stream on each side, which is itself all the time running at four or five miles an hour. But it is the positive speed of the current that ought really to be considered, for it is by this the boat will be urged against a breaker stationary in the river.

To get to this middle channel at once from the place where I had left my boat was not possible. I must enter it higher up the river, so I had to pull the canoe up stream, over shallows, and along the bristly margin, wading, towing, and struggling, for about half a mile, till at length it seemed I must be high enough up stream to let me paddle out swiftly across, while the current would take the boat sideways to the rough water.

In a little quiet bay I rested half an hour to recover strength after this exertion, and to prepare fully for a "spurt," which might be delayed in starting, but which, once begun, must be vigorous and all watchful to the end.

Here various thoughts blended and seemed to tumble about in the mind most disorderly. To leave this quiet bank and willingly rush out, in cold blood, into a field of white breakers; to tarnish the fair journey with a foolhardy prank; to risk the Rob Roy where the touch of one rock was utter destruction. Is it pleasant? Is it wise? Is it right?

The answer was, to sponge out every drop of water from the boat, to fasten the luggage inside, that it might not fall out in an upset, to brace the waterproof cover all tight around, and to get its edge in my teeth ready to let go in capsizing, and then to pull one gentle stroke which put the boat's nose out of the quiet water into the fast stream, and hurrah! we are off at a swinging pace.

The sun, now shining exactly up stream, was an exceedingly uncomfortable addition to the difficulties; for its glancing beams confounded all the horizon in one general band of light, so that rocks, waves, solid water, and the most flimsy foam were all the same at a little distance. This, the sole disadvantage of a cloudless sky, was so much felt in my homeward route that I sometimes prolonged the morning's work by three or four hours (with sun behind or on one side), so as to shorten the evening's *quota* where it was dead in the eye of the sun. On the present occasion, when it was of great moment to hit the channel exactly, I could not see it at all, even with my blue spectacles on. They seemed to be utterly powerless against such a fiery blaze; and, what was almost worse, the eye was thereby so dazzled that on looking to nearer objects I could scarcely see them either.

This unexpected difficulty was so serious that I thought for a moment of keeping on in my present course (directed straight across the river), so as to attain the opposite side, and there to wait for the sun to go down.

But it was already too late to adopt this plan, for the current had been swiftly bearing me down stream, and I had to come to an instant decision. "Now," thought I, "judging by the number of paddle-strokes, we must be opposite the channel in the middle, and now I must turn to it."

By a happy hit, the speed and the direction of the canoe were both well fitted, so that when the current had borne us to the breakers the boat's bow was just turned exactly down stream, and I entered the channel whistling for very loneliness, like a boy in the dark.

But it was soon seen to be "all right, Englishman;" so in ten minutes more the canoe had passed the rapids, and we floated along pleasantly on that confused "bobbery" of little billows always found below broken water,—a sort of mob of waves, which for a time seem to be elbowing and jostling in all directions to find their proper places.

I saw here two fishermen by one of the salmon traps described above, and at once pulled over to them, to land on a little white bank of sand, that I might rest, and bale out, and hear the news.

The men asked if I had come down the rapids in that boat. "Yes." "By the middle channel?" "Yes." They smiled to each other, and then both at once commenced a most voluble and loud-spoken address in the vilest of patois. Their eagerness and energy rose to such a pitch that I began to suppose they were angry; but the upshot of all this eloquence (always louder when you are seen not to understand one word of it) was this, "There are other rapids to come. You will get there in half an hour. They are far worse than what you have passed. Your boat *must* be carried round them on land."

To see if this was said to induce me to employ

them as porters, I asked them to come along in their boat, so as to be ready to help me; but they consulted together, and did not by any means agree in admiring this proposal. Then I asked them to explain the best route through the next rapids, when they drew such confused diagrams on the sand, and gave such complicated directions, that it was impossible to make head or tail of their atrocious jargon; so I quietly bowed, wiped out the sand pictures with my foot, and started again happy and free; for it is really the case that in these things "ignorance is bliss." The excitement of finding your way, and the satisfaction when you have found it yourself, is well worth all the trouble. Just so in mountain travel. If you go merely to work the muscles, and to see the view, it will do to be tied by a rope to three guides, and to follow behind them; but then *theirs* is all the mental exertion, and tact, and judgment, while yours is only the merit of keeping up with the leaders, treading in their steps. And therefore I have observed that there is less of this particular pleasure of the discoverer when one is ascending Mont Blanc, or other hills where one must be tied to the guides, than in making out a path over a mountain pass undirected, though the heights thus climbed up are not so great.

When the boat got near the lower rapids, I went ashore and walked for half a mile down the bank, and so was able to examine the bearings well. It appeared practicable to get along by the shallower parts of one side, so this was resolved upon as my course.

It is surely quite fair to go by the easiest way, provided there is no carrying overland adopted, or other plan for shirking the water. The method accordingly used in this case was rather a novel mode of locomotion, and it was quite successful, as well as highly amusing.

In the wide plain of breakers here, the central district seemed radically bad, so I cautiously kept out of the main current, and went where the stream ran fast enough nevertheless. I sat stridelegs on the deck of the boat near its stern, and was thus floated down until the bow, projecting out of the water, went above a ridge of rocks, and the boat grounded. Thus I received the shock against my legs (hanging in the water), so that the violence of its blow was eased off from the boat.

Then I immediately fixed both feet on the rock, and stood up, and the canoe went free from between my knees, and could be lowered down or pushed forward until the water got deeper, and when it got too deep to wade after her I pulled

"Astride the Stern."

the boat back between my knees, and sat down again on it as before.

The chief difficulty in this proceeding was to be equally attentive at once to keep hold of the boat, to guide it between rocks, to keep hold of the paddle, and to manage not to tumble on loose stones, or to get into the water above the waist.

Thus by successive riding and ferrying over the deep pools, and walking and wading in the shallows, by pushing the boat here, and by being carried upon it there, the lower rapids of Rheinfelden were most successfully passed without any damage.

It will be seen from the descriptions already given of the rapids at Bremgarten, and now of these two rapids on the Rhine, that the main difficulties are only for him who goes there uninformed, and that these can be avoided by examining them on the spot at the cost of a walk and a short delay. But the pleasure is so much enhanced by the whole thing being novel, that, unless for a man who wishes simply to *get past*, it is better to seek a channel for oneself, even if a much easier one has been found out by other people.

The town of Rheinfelden was now in view, and I begun to wonder how the English four-oar boat I had traced as far as Lauffenburg could have managed to descend the rapids just now passed. But I was informed this crew had not a very successful time of it, and that the boat being stove in or waterlogged the men had to come ashore and get her carried past the rapids for half-an-hour. If this turns out to be an incorrect account the blame will rest on the people at Bâle, who gave it; but in corroboration, the hotel folks mentioned that when the five shipwrecked Britons arrived there their clothes and baggage were all drenched, and the waiter said, with a malicious grin, that thereby his friend the washerwoman had earned twenty-seven francs in one night.

On the left bank of the river was a large building with a smooth gravel shore in front, to which I steered at once. This was the great salt-water baths of Rheinfelden—a favourite resort for crippled invalids. The salt rock in the earth beneath impregnates the springs with such an intensity of brine that eighty per cent. of fresh water has to be added before the saline mixture can be medicinally employed as a bath. If you take a glass of the water as it proceeds from the spring, and put a little salt in it, the salt will not dissolve, the water is already saturated. A drop of it put on your coat speedily dries up and leaves a white stain of minute crystals. In fact, this water seemed to me to be far more saline than even the water of the Dead Sea, which is in all conscience salt enough, as every one knows who has rubbed it on his face in that reeking-hot death-stricken valley of Jericho.

Though the shore was pleasant here and the water was calm, I found no one to welcome me now, and yet this was the only time I had reason to expect somebody to greet the arrival of the canoe. For in the morning a worthy German had told me he was going by train to Rheinfelden, and he would keep a look out for the canoe, and would surely meet me on the beach if I " ever got through the rapids." But I found afterwards that he *had* come there, and with his friends, too, and they had waited and waited till at last they gave up the Rob Roy as a lost vessel. Excellent man, he must have had some novel excuses to comfort his friends with as they retired, disappointed, after waiting in vain!

There was however, not far off, a poor woman washing clothes by the river, and thumping and bullying them with a wooden bludgeon as if her sole object was to smash up the bachelor's shirt-buttons. A fine boy of eight years old was with her, a most intelligent little fellow, whose quick eye at once caught sight of the Rob Roy as it dashed round the point into the smooth water of the bay, and landed me there a tired, tanned traveller, wet and warm.

This juvenile helped me more than any man ever did, and with such alacrity, too, and intelligence, and good humour, that I felt grateful to the boy. We spread out the sails to dry, and my socks and shoes in the sun, and sponged out the boat, and then dragged her up the high bank. Here, by good luck, I found two wheels on an axle left alone, for what purpose I cannot imagine; but I got a stick and fastened it to them as a pole, and then put the boat on this extemporized vehicle, and with the boy (having duly got permission from his mamma) soon pulled the canoe to the gates of the old town, and then rattling through the streets, even to the door of the hotel. A bright franc in the lad's hand made him start with amaze, but he instantly rose to the dignity of the occasion, and some dozens of other urchins formed an attentive audience as he narrated the events of the last half-hour, and ended always by showing the treasure in his hand, " and the Herr gave me this ! "

The Krone hotel here is very prettily situated. It is a large house, with balconies overlooking the water, and a babbling jet d'eau in its garden, which hangs over the river.

The stream flows fast, and retains evidence of having passed through troublous times higher up, therefore it makes no small noise as it rushes under the arches of the covered wooden bridge, but though there are rocks and a few eddies the passage is easy enough if you look at it for five minutes to form a mental chart of your course. My German friend having found out that the canoe had arrived after all, his excitement and pleasure abounded. Now he was proved right. Now his promises, broken as it seemed all day, were all fulfilled.

He was a very short, very fat, and very hilarious

personage, with a minute smattering of English, which he had to speak loudly, so as to magnify its value among his Allemand friends, envious of his accomplishment.

His explanations of the contents of my sketch-book were truly ludicrous as he dilated on it page by page, but he well deserved all gratitude for ordering my hotel bedroom and its comforts, which were never more acceptable than now after a hard day's work. Music finished the evening, and then the hum of the distant rapids sounded as I went to sleep.

Next morning, as there was but a short row to Bâle, I took a good long rest in bed, and then carried the canoe half way across the bridge where there is a picturesque island formed into a terraced garden, and here we launched the boat on the water. Although the knocks and strains of the last few days were very numerous, and many of them of portentous force, judging by the sounds they made, the Rob Roy was still hale and hearty, and the carpenter's mate had no damages to report to the captain. It was not until harder times came, in the remainder of the voyage, that her timbers suffered and her planks were tortured by rough usage.

A number of ladies patronized the start on this occasion, and as they waved their parasols and the men shouted hoch! and bravo! we glided down stream, the yellow paddle being waved round my head in an original mode of "salute," which I invented specially for returning friendly gratulations of this kind.

Speaking about Rheinfelden, Baedeker says, "Below the town another rapid of the Rhine forms a sort of whirlpool called the Höllenhaken," a formidable announcement, and a terrible name; but what is called here the "whirlpool" is not worth notice.

The sound of a railway train beside the river reminds you that this is not quite a strange, wild, unseen country. Reminds you I say, because really when you are in the river bed, you easily forget all that is beyond it on each side. Let a landscape be ever so well known from the road, it becomes new again when you view it from the level of the water. For before the scene was bounded by a semicircle with the diameter on the horizon, and the arch of sky for its circumference. But when you are seated in the canoe, the picture changes to the form of a great sector, with its point on the clear water, and each radius inclining aloft through rocks, trees, and mossy banks, on this side and on that. And this holds good even on a well worn river like the Thames. The landscenes between Oxford and London get pretty well known and admired by travellers, but the views will soon be fresh and fair if you row down the river through them. Nay, there are few rivers which have such lovely scenery as the Thames can show in its windings along that route.

But though the boat is not on the Thames it is now getting back to civilization, and away from that pleasant simplicity where everything done in the streets or the hotel is strange to a stranger, because it is natural to the natives. Here, on the contrary, we have composite candles and therefore no snuffers; here the waiter insists on speaking English, and sitting down by me, and clutching my arm, he confidentially informs me that there are no " bean green," translating "haricots verts," but that perhaps I might like a " flower caul," so I assent to a cauliflower.

This is funny enough, but far more amusing is it when the woman waiter of some inland German village shouts louder German to you, because that she rattles out at first is not understood. She gazes with a new sensation at a guest who actually cannot comprehend her voluble words, and then guest and waiter burst into laughter.

Here too I saw a boat towed along the Rhine —a painful evidence of being near commerce, even though it was in a primitive style; not that there was any towing-path, but men walked among the bushes, pulling the boat with a rope, and often wading to do so. This sight told me at once that I had left the fine free forests where you might land anywhere, and it was sure to be lonely and charming.

After a few bends westward we come in sight of the two towers of Bâle, but the setting sun makes it almost impossible to see anything in its brightness, so we must only paddle on.

The bridge at Bâle was speedily covered by the idle and the curious as the canoe pulled up at an hotel a few yards from the water.

It was here that the four-oared boat had arrived some weeks ago with its moist crew. The proprietor of the house was therefore much pleased to see another English boat come in, so little and so lonely, but still so comfortable and so dry. I walked about the town till I came to the Protestant church, where a number of people had assembled at a baptism. The baby was fixed on a sort of frame, so as to be easily handed about from mother to father, and from clerk to minister. I hereby protest against this mechanical arrangement as a flagrant indignity to the little darling. I have a great respect for babies, sometimes a certain awe. The instant the christening was done, a happy couple came forward to be married, an exceedingly clumsy dolt of a bridegroom and a fair bride, not very young, that is to say, about fifty-five years old. There were no bridesmaids or other perplexing appurtenances, and after the simple ceremony the couple just walked away, amid the titters of a numerous crowd of women. The bridegroom did not seem to know exactly what to do next. He walked before his wife, then behind her, and then on one side, but it did not somehow feel quite comfortable, so he assumed a sort of diagonal position, and kept nudging her on till they disappeared in some house. Altogether, I never saw a more unromantic commencement of married life, but there was this redeeming point, that they were not bored by that dread infliction— a marriage breakfast—the first meeting of two jealous sets of new relations, who are all expected to be made friends at once by eating when they are not hungry, and listening when there is nothing to say. But, come, it is not for an old bachelor to criticise these mysteries, so let us go back to the inn.

In the coffee-room a Frenchman, who had been in London, has just been instructing two Mexicans, who are going there, as to hotels, and it is excessively amusing to hear his description of the London "Caffy Hous," and the hotels in "Lycester-squar." "It is pronounced squar," he said, "in England."

CHAPTER XI.

Private concert—Thunderer—La Hardt Forest—River Ill—Madame Nico—Vosges—Admirers—New wine.

BALE is, in every sense, a turning-point on the Rhine. The course of the river here bends abruptly from west to north, and the character of the scenery beside it alters at once from high sloping banks to a widespread network of streams, all entangled in countless islands, and yet ever tending forward, northward, seaward through the great rich valley of the Rhine with mountain chains far off, but reared on each side like two everlasting barriers.

Here then I could start anew almost in any direction, and I had not settled yet what route to take, whether by the Saone and Doubs to paddle to the Rhone, and so descend to Marseilles, and coast by the Cornici road, and sell the boat at Genoa; or—and this second plan must be surely a better alternative, if by it we can avoid a sale of the Rob Roy—I could not part with her now—so let us at once decide to go back through France.

I was yet on the river slowly paddling when this decision was arrived at, and the river carried me still, for I determined not to leave its pleasant easy current for a slow canal, until the last possible opportunity. A diligent study of new maps procured at Bâle, showed that a canal ran northward nearly parallel to the Rhine, and approached very near to the river at one particular spot, which indeed looked hard enough to find even on the map, but was far more dubious when we got into a maze of streamlets and little rivers circling among high osiers, so thick and close that even on shore it was impossible to see a few yards.

But the line of tall poplars along the canal was visible now and then, so I made a guesswork turn, and it was not far wrong, or at any rate I got so near the canal that by winding about for a little in a pretty limpid stream, I brought the Rob Roy at last within carrying distance.

A song or two (without words) and a variation of the music by whistling on the fingers would be sure to bring anybody out of the osiers who was within reach of the outlandish concert, and so it proved, for a woman's head soon peered over a break in the dense cover. She wished to help to carry the boat herself, but the skipper's gallantry had scruples as to this proposal, so she disappeared and soon fetched a man, and we bore the canoe with some trouble through hedges and bushes, and over dykes and ditches, and at last through deep grassy fields, till she was safely placed on the canal.

The man was delighted by a two-franc piece. He had been well paid for listening to bad music, the reverse of the arrangement at ordinary concerts.

To my surprise and satisfaction the canal had a decided current in it, and in the right direction too. It is true that this current was only about two miles an hour, but even that is something.

This little channel was only about twelve feet wide, yet it was clear and deep, and by no means stupid to travel on.

After a few miles I came to a drawbridge, which rested within a foot of the water. A man came to raise the bridge by machinery, and he was surprised to see my way of passing it instead, that is, to shove my boat under it, while I quietly walked over it and got into the boat at the other side. This was, without doubt, the first boat which had traversed the canal without the bridge being raised, but I had passed several very low bridges on the Danube, some of them not two inches above the surface of the water. The very existence of these proves that no boats pass there, and mine only passed by pulling it over the bridge itself. It may be asked, how such a low bridge fares in flood times? and the answer is, that the water simply flows all over it. In some cases the planks which form the roadway are removed when the water rises, and then the wayfaring man who comes to the river must manage in some other mode. His bridge is removed at the very time when the high water makes it most necessary.

The bridge man was so intelligent in his remarks that I determined to stop there and breakfast, so I left the canoe in his charge and found my way to a little publichouse at the hamlet of Gros Kembs, and helped the wizened old lady who ruled there to make me an omelette—my help, by the bye, consisted in ordering, eating, and paying for the omelette, for the rest she was sure to do well enough, as all French women can, and no English ones.

The village gossips soon arrived, and each person who saw the boat came on to the inn to see the foreigner who could sail in such a *bateau*.

The courteous and respectful behaviour of Continental people is so uniform that the stranger among them is bound, I think, to amuse and interest these folk in return. This was most easily done by showing all my articles of luggage,* and of course the drawings. A Testament with gilt leaves was, however, the chief object of curiosity, and all the savants of the party tried in turn to read it.

One of these as spokesman, and with commendable gravity, told me he had read in their district newspaper about the canoe, but he little expected to have the honour of meeting its owner.

Fancy the local organ of such a place! Is it called the "News of the Wold," or the "Gros Kembs Thunderer"? Well, whatever was the title of the Gazette, it had an article about Pontius Pilate and my visit to the Titisee in the Black Forest, and this it was no doubt which made these canal people so very inquisitive on the occasion.

The route now lay through the great forest of La Hardt, with dense thickets on each side of the canal, and not a sound anywhere to be heard but the hum now and then of a dragon fly.

One or two woodmen met me as they trudged silently home from work, but there was a lonely feeling about the place without any of the romance of wild country. In the most brilliant day the scenery of a canal has at best but scant liveliness, the whole thing is so prosaic and artificial, and in

* See an inventory of these in the Appendix.

fact stupid, if one can ever say that of any place where there is fresh air and clear water, and blue sky and green trees.

Still I had to push on, and sometimes, for a change, to tow the boat while I walked. The difference between a glorious river encircling you with lofty rocks and this canal with its earthen walls was something like that between walking in a valley among high mountains and being shut up by mistake in Bloomsbury-square.

No birds chirped or sung, or even flew past, only the buzzing of flies was mingled with the distant shriek of a train on the railway. It is this railway which has killed the canal, for I saw no boats moving upon it. The long continued want of rain had also reduced its powers of accommodation for traffic, and the traffic is so little at the best that it would not pay to buy water for the supply. For in times of drought canal water is very expensive. It was said that the Regent's Canal, in London, had to pay 5,000*l.* for what they required last summer, in consequence of the dryness of the season.

At length we came to a great fork of the canal in a wide basin, and I went along the branch to the town of Mulhouse, a place of great wealth, the largest French cotton town—the Manchester of France.

The street boys here were very troublesome, partly because they were intelligent, and therefore inquisitive, and partly because manufacturing towns make little urchins precocious and forward in their manners.

I hired a truck from a woman and hired a man to drag it, and so took the boat to the best hotel, a fine large house, where they at once recognized the canoe, and seemed to know all about it from report.

The hotel porter delayed so long next morning to wheel the boat to the railway, that when I took her into the luggage office as usual and placed the boat on the counter with the trunks and bandboxes, the officials declined to put it in the train.

This was the first time it had been refused on a railroad, and I used every kind of persuasion, but in vain, and this being the first application of the kind on French soil I felt that difficulties were ahead, if this precedent was to hold good.

Subsequent experience showed that the French railways will not take a canoe as baggage; while the other seven or eight countries I had brought the boat through were all amenable to pressure on this point.

I had desired to go by the railway only a few miles, but it would have enabled me to avoid about fifty locks on the canal and thus have saved two tedious days. As, however, they would not take the boat in a passenger train I carried her back to the canal, and I determined to **face** the locks boldly, and to regard them as an exercise of patience and of the flexor muscles, as it happens sometimes one's walk is only " a constitutional."

The Superintendent of the Rhine and Rhone Canal was very civil, and endeavoured to give me the desirable information I required, but which he had not got, that is to say, the length, depth, and general character of the several rivers I proposed to navigate in connexion with streams less "canalizé," so I had to begin again as usual, without any knowledge of the way.

With rather an ill-tempered "adieu" to Mulhouse, the Rob Roy set off again on its voyage. The water assumed quite a new aspect, now that one *must* go by it, but it was not so much the water as the locks which were objectionable. For at each of these there is a certain form of operations to be gone through—all very trifling and without variety, yet requiring to be carefully performed, or you may have the boat injured, or a ducking for yourself.

When I get to a lock I have to draw to the bank, open my waterproof covering, put my package and paddle ashore, then step out and haul the boat out of the water. By this time two or three persons usually congregate. I select the most likely one, and ask him to help in such a persuasive but dignified manner that he feels it an honour to carry one end of the boat while I take the other, and so we put her in again above the barrier, and, if the man looks poor, I give him a few sous. At some of the locks they asked me for a "carte de permission," or pass for travelling on their canal, but I laughed the matter off, and when they pressed it with a "mais monsieur," I kept treating the proposal as a good joke, until the officials were fairly baffled and gave in. The fact is, I had got into the canal as one gets over the hedge on to a public road, and as I did not use any of the water in locks or any of the lock-keepers' time, and the "pass" was a mere form, price 5*d*., it was but reasonable to go unquestioned; and besides, this "carte" could not be obtained except at the beginning. Having set off late, I went on until about sunset, when we passed into the **river Ill**, a long dull stream, which flows through the Vosges into the Rhine.

This stream was now quite stagnant, and a mere collection of pools covered by thick scum. It was therefore a great comfort to have only a short voyage upon it.

When I got back again to the canal, an

acquaintance was formed with a fine young lad, who was reading as he sauntered along. He was reading of canoe adventures in America, and so I got him to walk some miles beside me, and to help the boat over some locks, telling him he could thus see how different actual canoeing was from the book stories about it made up of romance! He was pining for some expansion of his sphere, and specially for foreign travel, and above all to see England. We went to an *auberge*, where I ordered a bottle of wine, the cost of which was twopence halfpenny. After he left, and as it grew dark, I halted, put my boat in a lock-keeper's house, and got his son to conduct me to the little village of Illfurth, a most unsophisticated place indeed, with a few vineyards on a hill behind it, though the railway has a road station near. It was not easy to mistake which was the best house here even in the dark, so I inquired of madame at the White Horse if she could give me a bed. "Not in a room for one alone; three others will be sleeping in the same chamber."

This she had answered after glancing at my puny package and travel-worn dress, but her ideas about the guest were enlarged when she heard of how he had come, and so she managed (they always do if you give time and smiles and show sketches) to allot me a nice little room to myself, with two beds of the hugest size, a water-jug of the most minute dimensions, and sheets very coarse and very clean. Another omelette was consumed while the customary visitors surrounded the benighted traveller; carters, porters, all of them with courteous manners, and behaving so well to me and to one another, and talking such good sense, as to make me feel how different from this is the noisy taproom of a roadside English "public."

Presently two fine fellows of the Gendarmerie came in for their half bottle of wine, at one penny, and as both of them had been in the Crimea there was soon ample subject for most interesting conversation. This was conducted in French, but the people here usually speak a patois utterly impossible for one to comprehend. I found they were discussing me under various conjectures, and settled at last that I must be rather an odd fish, but certainly a gentleman, and probably "noble." They were most surprised to hear I meant to stop all the next day at Illfurth, simply because it was Sunday, but they did not fail to ask for my passport, which until this I had carried about without having had a single inquiry on the subject.

The sudden change from a first-rate hotel this

P

morning to the roadside inn of Illfurth, was more entertaining on account of its variety than for its agreeables; but in good health and good weather one can put up with anything.

The utter silence of peaceful and cool night in a place like this reigns undisturbed until about four o'clock in early morn, when the first sound is some matutinal cock, who crows first because he is proud of being first awake. After he has asserted his priority thus once or twice, another deeper toned rooster replies, and presently a dozen cocks are all in full song, and in different keys. In half an hour you hear a man's voice; next, some feminine voluble remarks; then a latch is moved and clicks, the dog gives a morning bark, and a horse stamps his foot in the stable because the flies have aroused to breakfast on his tender skin. At length a pig grunts, his gastric juice is fairly awake, the day is begun. And so the stream of life, thawed from its sleep, flows gently on again, and at length the full tide of village business is soon in agitation, with men's faces and women's quite as full of import as if this French Stoke Pogis were the capital of the world.

While the inmates prepare for early mass, and my bowl of coffee is set before me, there are four dogs, eight cats, and seven canaries (I counted them) all looking on, moving, twittering, mewing, each evidently sensible that a being from some other land is present among them; and as they look with doubtful inquiring eyes on the stranger, there is felt more strongly by him too, "Yes, I am in a foreign country."

On Sunday I had a quiet rest, and walk, and reading, and an Englishman, who had come out for a day from Mulhouse to fish, dined in the pleasant arbour of the inn with his family. One of his girls managed to fall into a deep pond and was nearly drowned, but I heard her cries, and we soon put her to rights. This Briton spoke with quite a foreign accent, having been six years in France; but his Lancashire dialect reappeared in conversation, and he said he had just been reading about the canoe in a Manchester paper. His children had gone that morning to a Sunday-school before they came out by railway to fish in the river here; but I could not help contrasting their rude manners with the good behaviour of the little "lady and gentleman" children of my host. One of these, Philibert, was very intelligent, and spent an hour or two with me, so we became great friends. He asked all kinds of questions about England and America, far more than I was able to answer. I gave him a little book with a picture in it, that he might read it to his father, for it contained the remarkable conversation between Napoleon and his Marshal at St. Helena concerning the Christian religion, a paper well worth reading, whoever spoke the words. This Sunday being an annual village fête a band played, and some very uncouth couples waltzed the whole day. Large flocks of sheep, following their shepherds, wandered over the arid soil. The poor geese, too, were flapping their wings in vain as they tried to swim in water an inch deep, where usually there had been pleasant pools in the river. I sympathized with the geese, for I missed my river sadly too.

My bill here for the two nights, with plenty to eat and drink, amounted to five shillings in all, and I left Madame Nico with some regret, starting again on the canal, which looked more dull and dirty than before.

After one or two locks this sort of travelling became so insufferable that I suddenly determined to change my plans entirely—for is not one free? By the present route several days would be consumed in going over the hills by a series of tedious locks; besides, this very canal had been already traversed by the four-oar boat Waterwitch some years ago. A few moments of thought, and I got on the bank to look for some way of deliverance. Far off I could see the vine-clad hills of the Vosges, and I decided at once to leave the canal, cross the country to those hills, cart the canoe over the range, and so reach the source of the Moselle, and thus begin to paddle on quite another set of rivers. I therefore turned my prow back, went down the canal, and again entered the river Ill, but soon found it too shallow to float even my canoe. Once more I retraced my way, ascending the locks, and, passing by Illfurth, went on to reach a village where a cart could be had. Desperation made me paddle hard even in the fierce sun, but it was not that which so much troubled me as the humiliation of thus rowing back and forward for miles on a dirty, stagnant canal, and passing by the same locks two or three times, with the full conviction that the people who gazed at the procedure must believe me not only to be mad (this much one can put up with), but furiously insane, and dangerous to be at large.

Whether we confess it or not we all like to be admired. The right or wrong of this depends on for what and from whom we covet admiration. But when the deed you attract attention by is no longer a great one, or one which others have not done or cannot do, but is one that all other people could but would not do, then you are not admired as remarkable but only stared at as singular.

214 METAPHYSICS.

The shade of a suspicion that this is so in any act done before lookers-on is enough to make it hateful. Nay, you have then the sufferings of a martyr, without his cause or his glory. But I fear that instead of getting a cart for the canoe I am getting out of depth in metaphysics, which means, you know, "When ane maun explains till anither what he disna understaun himsel, that's metapheesics."

Well, when we came to the prescribed village, named Haidwiller, I found they had plenty of carts, but not one would come to help me even for a good round sum. It was their first day with the grapes, and "ancient customs must be observed"; but I went on still further to another village, and here I found them letting out the water from the canal to repair a lock. Here was a position of unenviable repose for the poor Rob Roy! No water to float in, and no cart to carry her.

To aid deliberation I attacked a large cake of hot flour baked by the lock-keeper's dirty wife, and we stuck plums in it to make it go down, while I sent the man to the fields to get some animal that could drag a clumsy vehicle—cart is too fine a name for it—which I had impressed from a ploughman near.

The man came back leading a gloomy-looking

BOAT CART. 215

"The Rob Roy on wheels."

bullock, and we started with the boat now travelling on wheels, but at a most dignified pace.*

This was the arrangement till we reached another village, where there were no vineyards, and therefore I could get a horse there, instead of the gruff bullock; while the natives were lost in amazement to see a boat in a cart, and a big foreigner gabbling beside it.

* The sketch represents the lady cow which dragged the cart at Lauffenburg, but it will do almost equally well for the present equipage.

The sun was exceedingly hot, and the road dusty; but I felt the walk would be a pleasant change, though my driver kept muttering to himself about my preference of pedestrianism to the fearful jolts of his cart.

We passed thus through several villages on a fine fruitful plain, and at some of them the horse had to bait, or the driver to lunch, or his employer to refresh the inner man, in every case the population being favoured with an account by the driver of all he knew about the boat, and a great deal more.

At one of the inns on the road some new wine was produced on the table. It had been made only the day before, and its colour was exactly like that of cold tea, with milk and sugar in it, while its taste was very luscious and sweet. This new wine is sometimes in request, but especially among the women. "Corn shall make the young men cheerful, and new wine the maids." (Zech. ix. 17.)

CHAPTER XII.

Bonfire — My wife — Matthews — Tunnel picture — Imposture — Moselle — Cocher — Gymnastics — The paddle — A spell — Overhead — Feminine forum.

As evening came on the little flag of the Rob Roy, which was always hoisted, even in a cart, showed signs of animation, being now revived by a fresh breeze from the beautiful Vosges mountains when we gradually brought their outline more distinctly near.

Then we had to cross the river Thur, but that was an easy matter in these scorched days of drought. So the cavalcade went on till, the high road being reached, we drove the cart into the pretty town of Thann. The driver insisted on going to *his* hotel, but when I got there I saw it could not be the best in a town of this size (experience quickens perception in these matters), and I simply took the reins, backed out of the yard, and drove to a better one.

Here the hotel-keeper had read of the Rob Roy, so it was received with all the honours, and the best of his good things was at my disposal.

In the evening I burned some magnesium-wire signals to amuse the rustics, who came in great crowds along the roads, drawing home their bullock-carts, well loaded with large vats full of the new grapes, and singing hoarsely as they waved aloft flowers and garlands and danced around them,—the rude rejoicings for a bounteous vine harvest. It is remarkable how soon the good singing of Germany is lost trace of when you cross into France, though the language of the peasants here was German enough.

At night I went to see an experiment in putting out fires. A large bonfire was lighted in the market-place, and the inventor of the new apparatus came forward, carrying on his back a vessel full of water, under the pressure of "six atmospheres" of carbonic acid gas. He directed this on the fire from a small squirt at the end of a tube, and it was certainly most successful in immediately extinguishing the flames.* This gentleman and other *savants* of the town then visited the boat, and the usual entertainment of the sketch-book closed a pleasant day, which had begun with every appearance of being the reverse.

Although this is a busy place, I found only one

---

* This invention has since been exhibited in London, and it seems to be a valuable one.

book-shop in it, and that a very bad one. A priest and two nuns were making purchases there, and I noticed that more images and pictures than printed books were kept for sale.

Next morning a new railroad enabled me to take the boat a little farther into the hills; but they fought hard to make her go separate, that is, in a "merchandise" train, though I said the boat was "my wife," and could not travel alone. At last they put their wise heads together, filled up five separate printed forms, charged double fare, and the whole thing cost me just ninepence. Verily, the French are still overloaded with forms, and are still in the straitwaistcoat of *système*. The railway winds among green hills, while here and there a "fabrik," or factory, nestles in a valley, or illumines a hill-side at night with its numerous windows all lighted up. These are the chief depôts of that wonderful industry of taste which spreads the shawls and scarfs of France before the eyes of an admiring world, for ladies to covet, and for their husbands to buy. I was informed that the designs for patterns here cost large sums, as if they were the oil paintings of the first masters, and that three times as much is paid here for cutting one in wood as will be given by an English manufacturer. At Wesserling I managed to mount the Rob Roy on a spring vehicle, and we set off gaily up the winding road that passes the watershed of the Vosges mountains. I never had a more charming drive. For six hours we were among woods, vineyards, bright rivulets, and rich pastures. Walking up a hill, I overtook a carriage, and found one of the occupants was an Englishman. But he had resided in France for more than twenty years, and really I could scarcely understand his English. He spoke of "dis ting," and "ve vill go," and frequently mingled French and German words with his native tongue. In a newspaper article here I noticed after the name "Matthews," the editor had considerately added, "pronounced, in English, Massious." This is well enough for a Frenchman, but it certainly is difficult to conceive how a man can fail in pronouncing our "th," if he is a real live Englishman. When he found out my name, he grasped my hand, and said how deeply interested he had been in a tract written by one of the same name, giving an account of the "Loss of the Kent East Indiaman by Fire."

The spring carriage had been chartered as an expensive luxury in this cheap tour, that is to say, my boat and myself were to be carried about thirty-five miles in a comfortable four-wheeled vehicle for twenty-six francs—not very dear when you consider that it saved a whole day's time to me and a whole day's jolting to the canoe, which seemed to enjoy its soft bed on the top of the cushion, and to appreciate very well the convenience of springs. After a good hard pull up a winding road we got to the top of the pass of this "little Switzerland," as it is called, and here was a tunnel on the very crest of the watershed.

The arch of this dark tunnel made an excellent frame to a magnificent picture; for before me was stretched out broad France. All streams at our back went down to the all-absorbing Rhine, but those in front would wend their various ways, some to the Mediterranean, others into the Bay of Biscay, and the rest into the British Channel.

A thousand peaks and wooded knolls were on this side and that, while a dim panorama of five or six villages and sunny plains extended before us. This was the chain of the Vosges mountains and their pleasant vales, where many valorous men have been reared. The most noted crusaders came from this district, and from here too the first of the two great Napoleons drew the best soldiers of his army.* Most of the community are Protestants.

High up on one side of us was a pilgrim station, where thousands of people come year by year, and

* The giant called "Anak," who is now exhibiting in London, is from the Vosges mountains.

probably they get fine fresh air and useful exercise. The French seem to walk farther for superstitious purposes than for mere pedestrian amusement.*

My English friend got into my carriage, and we drove a little way from the road to the village of Bussang to see the source of the Moselle.

This river rises under the "Ballon d'Alsace," a lofty mountain with a rounded top, and the stream consists at first of four or five very tiny trickling rivulets which unite and come forth in a

---

* Among other celebrated French "stations" there is the mountain of La Salette, near Grenoble, where, even in one day, 16,000 pilgrims have ascended to visit the spot where the Virgin Mary was said to have spoken to some shepherds. On the occasion of my pilgrimage there I met some donkeys with panniers bringing down holy water (in lemonade bottles) which was sold throughout Europe for a shilling a bottle, until a priest at the bottom of the mountain started a private pump of his own. The woman who had been hired to personate the Holy Saint confessed the deception, and it was exploded before the courts of law in a report which I read on the spot; but the Roman Catholic papers, even in England, published attractive articles to support this flagrant imposture, and its truth and goodness were vehemently proclaimed in a book by the Romish Bishop of Birmingham, with the assent of the Pope. Methinks it is easier to march barefoot 100 miles over sharp stones than to plod your honest walk of life on common pavement and with strong soled boots.

little spring well about the size of a washing-tub, from which the water flows across the road in a channel that you can bridge with your fingers.

But this bubbling brook had great interest for me, as I meant to follow its growth until it would be strong enough to bear me on its cool, clear water, now only like feathers strewed among the grass, and singing its first music very pretty and low.

We like to see the source of a great river; a romantic man must have much piquant thought at the sight, and a poetic man must be stirred by its sentiment. Every great thought must also have had a source or germ, and it would be interesting to know how and when some of the grand ideas that have afterwards aroused nations first quivered in the brain of a genius, a warrior, a philosopher, or a statesman. And besides having a source, each stream of thought has a current too, with ripples and deep pools, and scenery as it were around. Some thoughts are lofty, others broad; some are straight, and others round about; some are rushing, while others glide peacefully; only a few are clear and deep.

But this is not the place to launch upon fancy's dreams, or even to describe the real, pretty valleys around us in the Vosges. We go through these merely to find water for the Rob Roy, and in this search we keep descending every hour.

When the bright stars came out I saw them glitter below thick trees in pools of the water now so quickly become a veritable river, and I scanned each lagoon in the darkness to know if still it was too small for the boat.

We came to the town of Remiremont and to a bad sort of inn, where all was disorder and dirt. The driver sat down with me to a late supper and behaved with true French politeness, which always shows better in company than in private, or when real self-denial or firm friendship is to be tested. So he ate of his five different courses, and had his wine, fruit, and neat little etceteras, and my bill next day for our united entertainment and lodging was just 3s. 4d.

This *cocher* was an intelligent man, and conversed on his own range of subjects with considerable tact, and when our conversation was turned upon the greater things of another world he said, "They must be happy there, for none of them have ever come back"—a strange thought, oddly phrased. As he became interested in the subject I gave him a paper upon it, which he at once commenced to read aloud.*

* Some days previously a stranger gave me a bundle of papers to read, for which I thanked him much. When I

Next morning, the 20th of September, the Rob Roy was brought to the door in a handcart, and was soon attended by its usual levee.

As we had come into the town late at night the gazers were ignorant of any claims this boat might have upon their respect, and some of them derided the idea of its being able to float on the river here, or at any rate to go more than a mile or two.

But I had previously taken a long walk before breakfast to examine the Moselle, and I was convinced it could be begun even here and in this dry season. A curious old gentleman, with green spectacles and a white hat, soon brought the sceptical mob to their senses by telling them he had read often about the boat, and they must not make fun of it now.

Then they all chopped round and changed their minds in a moment—the fickle French—and they helped me with a will, and carried the Rob Roy

was at leisure I examined the packet, which consisted of about thirty large pages sewn together, and comprising tracts upon politics, science, literature, and religion. The last subject was most prominent, and was dealt with in a caustic clever style, which interested me very much. These tracts were printed in England and with good paper and type. They are a weekly series, distributed everywhere at six shillings a dozen, and each page is entitled "The Saturday Review."

about a mile to the spot fixed upon for the start, which was speedily executed, with a loud and warm "Adieu!" and "Bon voyage!" from all the spectators.

It was pleasant again to grasp the paddle and to find pure clear water below, which I had not seen since the Danube, and to have a steady current alongside that was so much missed on the Ill and the Basel Canal.

Pretty water flowers quivered in the ripples round the mossy stones, and park-like meadows sloped to the river with fruit trees heavy laden. After half an hour of congratulation that I had come to the Moselle rather than the Saone and the Doubs, I settled down to my day's work with cheerfulness.

The water of this river was very clear and cool, meandering through long deep pools, and then over gurgling shallows; and the fish, waterfowl, woods, and lovely green fields were a most welcome change from the canal I had left. The sun was intensely hot, but the spare "jib," as a shawl on my shoulders, defied its fierce rays, and so I glided along in solitary enjoyment. The numerous shallows required much activity with the paddle, and my boat got more bumped and thumped to-day than in any other seven days of the tour. Of course I had often to get out and to tow her through the water; sometimes through the fields, or over rocks, but this was easily done with canvas shoes on, and flannel trousers that are made for constant ducking.

The aspect of the river was rather of a singular character for some miles, with low banks sloping backwards, and richly carpeted with grass, so that the view on either side was ample; but there was also in front a spacious picture of several successive levels, seen to great advantage from the great height we were upon, and from which the river descends by sudden leaps and deep falls, chiefly artificial, and some trouble is caused in getting down each of these. The boat had to be lowered by hand, with a good deal of gymnastic exercise among the slippery rocks; the mosses and lichens were studied in anything but botanical order.

At this period of the voyage the paddle felt so natural in my hands from long use of it every day, that it was held unconsciously. In the beginning of my practice I had invented various tethers and ties to secure this all-important piece of furniture from being lost if it should fall overboard, and I had practised what ought to be done if the paddle should be ever beaten out of hand by a wave, or dropped into the water in a moment of carelessness.

But none of these plans were satisfactory in actual service. The strings got entangled when I jumped out suddenly, or I forgot the thing was tied when I had to throw it out on the shore, so it was better to have the paddle perfectly loose; and thus free, it never was dropped or lost hold of even in those times of difficulty or confusion which made twenty things to be done, and each to be done first, when an upset was imminent, and a jump out had to be managed instead.*

The movement of the paddle, then, got to be almost involuntary, just as the legs are moved in walking, and the ordinary difficulties of a river seemed to be understood by the mind without special observation, and to be dealt with naturally, without hesitation or reasoning as to what ought to be done. This faculty increased until long gazes upwards to the higher grounds or to the clouds were fully indulged without apparently

---

* The bamboo mast was meant originally to serve also as a boat-hook or hitcher, and had a ferrule and a fishing gaff neatly fastened on the end, which fitted also into the mast step. I recollect having used the boat-hook once at Gravesend, but it was instantly seen to be a mistake. You don't want a boat-hook when your canoe can come close alongside where it is deep, and will ground when it is shallow. Besides, to use a boat-hook you must drop the paddle.

interrupting the steady and proper navigation of the boat, even when it was moving with speed. On one of these occasions I had got into a train of thought on this subject, and was regretting that the course of the stream made me turn my back on the best scenery. I had spun round two or three times to feast my eyes once more and again upon some glowing peaks, lit up by the setting sun, until a sort of fascination seized the mind, and a quiet lethargy crept over the system; and, moreover, a most illogical persuasion then settled that the boat always *did* go right, and that it was no use being so much on the alert to steer well. This still held me as I came into a cluster of about a dozen rocks all dotted about, and with the stream welling over this one and rushing over that, and yet I was spellbound and doggedly did nothing to guide the boat's course.

But the water was avenged on this foolish defiance of its power, for in a moment I was driven straight on a great rock, only two inches below the surface, and the boat at once swung round, broadside on to the current, and then slowly but determinedly began to turn over. As it canted more and more my lax muscles were rudely aroused to action, for the plain fact stared out baldly that I was about to get a regular ducking, and all from a stupid, lazy fit.

The worst of it was I was not sitting erect, but stretched almost at full length in the boat, and one leg was entangled inside by the strap of my bag. In the moments following (that seem minutes in such a case) I had a whole gush of thoughts through the mind while the poor little boat was still turning over, until at last I gave a spring from my awkward position to jump into the water.

The jerk released the canoe from the rock, and I only fell with head and arms into the river in a most undignified position, which had to be laughed off, as well as might be, when I recovered my seat, with a wet head and dripping sleeves!

However, this little *faux pas* quite wakened and sobered me, and I looked in half shame to the bank to see if any person had witnessed the absurd performance. And it was well to have done with sentiment and reveries, for the river had now got quite in earnest about going along.

Permit me again to invite attention to the washerwomen on the river. This institution, which one does not find thus floating on our streams in England, becomes a very frequent object of interest if you canoe it on the Continent.

As the well in Eastern countries is the recognised place for gossiping, and in colder climes a good deal of politics is settled in the barber's

"Washing Barge."

shop, so here in fluvial districts the washing barge is the forum of feminine eloquence.

The respectability of a town as you approach it is shadowed forth by the size and ornaments of the *blanchisseuses'* float; and as there are often fifty faces seen at once, the type of female loveliness may be studied for a district at a time. While they wash they talk, and while they talk they thump and belabour the clothes; but there is always some idle eye wandering which speedily will catch sight of the Rob Roy canoe.

In smaller villages, and where there is no barge

for them to use, the women have to do without one, and kneel on the ground, so that even in far-off parts of the river we shall find them there.

A flat sounding whack! whack! tells me that round the corner I shall come upon at least a couple of washerwomen, homely dames, with brown faces and tall caps, who are wringing, slapping, and scrubbing the "linge." Though this may encourage the French cotton trade, I rejoice that my own shirts are of strong woollen stuff, which defies their buffeting.

I always fraternized with these ladies, doffing my hat, and drawing back my left foot for a bow (though the graceful action is not observed under the macintosh). Other travellers, also, will find there is much to be seen and heard worth stopping for if they pass five minutes at the washing-barge. But even if it were not instructive and amusing thus to study character when a whole group is met with at once, surely it is to be remembered that the pleasure of seeing a new sight and of hearing a foreigner speak cheerful and kind words, is to many of these hard-working, honest mothers a bright interlude in a life of toil; and to give pleasure is one of the best pleasures of a tourist. It is in acting thus, too, that the lone traveller feels no loneliness, while he pleases and is pleased. Two Englishmen may travel together agreeably among foreigners for a week without learning so much of the life, and mind, and manners of the people as would be learned in one day if each of the tourists went alone, provided he was not too shy or too proud to open his eyes, and ears, and mouth among strangers, and had sense enough to be an exception to the rule that " Every Englishman is an island."

Merely for a change, I ran the Rob Roy into a long millrace in search of breakfast. A fine boy of twelve years old soon trotted alongside, and I asked him if he was an honest lad, which he answered by a blush, and " Yes." " Here is a franc, then. Go and buy me bread and wine, and meet me at the mill." A few of the " hands" soon found out the canoe, moored, as it was thought, in quiet retirement, with its captain resting under a tree, and presently a whole crowd of them swarmed out, and shouted with delight as they pressed round to see.

The boy brought a very large bottle of wine, and a loaf big enough to dine four men; and I set to work with an oarsman's appetite, and that happy *sang froid* which no multitude of gazers now could disturb.

However, one of the party invited me into her house, and soon set delicate viands before the new guest, while the others filled the room in an instant, and were replaced by sets of fifty at a time, all very good-humoured and respectful.

But it was so hot and bustling here that I resolved to go away and have a more pleasant and sulky meal by myself on some inaccessible island. The retreat through the crowd had to be regularly prepared for by military tactics; so I appointed four of the most troublesome boys as "policemen" to guard the boat in its transit across the fields, but they discharged their new duties with such vigour that two little fellows were soon knocked over into the canoe, and so I launched off, while the Manager of the factory called in vain to his cottonspinners, who were all now in full cry after the boat, and were making holiday without leave.

CHAPTER XIII.

Epinal—The Tramp—Halcyon—Painted woman—Beating to quarters—Boat in a hedge—The Meurthe—Moving House—Tears of a mother—Five francs.

IN a dark arbour-like arch of foliage, where the water was deep and still, I made fast to the long grass, cast my tired limbs into the fantastic contortions of ease, and, while the bottle lasted and the bread, I watched the bees and butterflies, and the beetles and rats, and the coloured tribes of airy and watery life that one can see so well in a quiet half hour like this.

How little we are taught at school about these wondrous communities of real life, each with its laws and instincts, its beauties of form, and marvellous ingenuities!

How little of flowers and insects, not to say of trees and animals, a boy learns as school-lessons, while he is forced at one end and crammed at the other with the complicated politics of heathen gods, and their loves and faction fights, which are neither real nor possible.

The Moselle rapidly enlarged in volume, though

one could easily see that it had seldom been so low before. It is a very beautiful river to row on, especially where I began it. Then it winds to the west and north, and again, turning a little eastwards, traverses a lovely country between Treves and Coblentz, where it joins the ancient Rhine.

My resting-place for this evening was Epinal, a town with little to interest; and so I could turn to books and pencils until it was time for bed.

Next day the scenery was by no means so attractive, but I had plenty of hard work, which was enjoyed very much, my shoes and socks being off all day, for it was useless to put them on when so many occasions required me to jump out.

Here it was a plain country, with a gravel soil, and fast rushings of current; and then long pools like the Serpentine, and winding turns leading entirely round some central hill which the river insisted upon circumventing.

At noon I came upon a large number of labourers at work on a milldam, and as this sort of crowd generally betokens something to eat (always, at any rate, some drinkable fluid), I left my boat boldly in mid-stream, and knocked at a cottage, when an old woman came out. "Madame, I am hungry, and you are precisely the lady who can make me an omelette." "Sir, I have nothing to give you." "Why," said I, "look at these hens; I am sure they have laid six eggs this morning, they look so proud." She evidently thought I was a tramp demanding alms, and when I told her to see the boat I had come in from England, she said she was so old she was too blind to see. However, we managed to make an omelette together, and she stood by (with an eye, perhaps, to her only fork) and chatted pleasantly, asking, "What have you got to sell?" I told her I had come there only for pleasure. "What sort of pleasure, Monsieur, can you possibly hope to find in *this* place?" But I was far too gallant to say bluntly that her particular mansion was not the ultimate object of the tour. After receiving a franc for the rough breakfast, she kept up a battery of blessings till I got to the boat, and ended by shrieking out to a navvy looking on, "I tell you every Englishman is rich!"

Next day was bright and blue-skyed as before, and an early start got the fine fresh morning air on the river.

The name of this river is sometimes pronounced "Moselle," and at other times "Mosel," what we should call "Mozle." When a Frenchman speaks of "la Moselle," he puts an equal emphasis on each of the three syllables he is pronouncing; whereas generally we Englishmen call this river the Mosélle.

The name of a long river goes through some changes as it traverses various districts and dialects; as, for instance, the Missouri, which you hear the travellers in Kansas call "Mzoory," while they wend along the Californian road.

When the scenery is tame, and the channel of the river is not made interesting by dangers to be avoided, then one can always turn again to the animals and birds, and five minutes of watching will be sure to see much that is curious. Here, for instance, we have the little kingfisher again, who meets us on the Danube and the Reuss, and whom we knew well in England before; but now we are on a visit to *his* domain, and we see him in his private character alone. There are several varieties of this bird, and they differ in form and colour of plumage. This "Royal bird," the *Halcyon* of antiquity, the *Alcedo* in classic tongue, is called in German "Eis fogl," or "Ice bird," perhaps because he fishes even in winter's frost, or because his nest is like a bundle of icicles, being made of minnows' bones most curiously wrought together.

But now it is on a summer day, and he is perched on a twig within two inches of the water, and under the shade of a briar leaf, his little parasol.

He is looking for fish, and is so steady that

you may easily pass him without observing that brilliant back of azure, or the breast of blushing red.

When I desired to see these birds, I quietly moved my boat till it grounded on a bank, and, after it was stationary thus for a few minutes, the Halcyon fisher got quite unconcerned, and plied his task as if unseen.

He peers with knowing eye into the shallow below him, and now and then he dips his head a bit to make quite sure he has marked a fish worth seizing; then suddenly he darts down with a splash, and flies off with a little white minnow, or a struggling sticklebat nipped in his beak.

If it is caught thus crosswise, the winged fisherman tosses his prey into the air, and nimbly catches it in his mouth, so that it may be gulped down properly. Then he quivers and shakes with satisfaction, and quickly speeds to another perch, flitting by you with wonderful swiftness, as if a sapphire had been flung athwart the sunbeam, flashing beauteous colours in its flight.

Or, if bed-time has come, or he is fetching home the family dinner, he flutters on and on, and then with a little sharp note of "good-bye," pops into a hole, the dark staircase to his tiny nest, and there he finds Mrs. Halcyon sitting in state, and thirteen **baby Kingfishers** gaping for the dainty fish.

This pretty **bird has an air** of quiet mystery, beauty, **and** vivid motion, all combined, which has made him a favourite with **the Rob Roy.**

Strangely enough, the river in this **part** of its course actually gets less and less as you descend it. Every few miles some of the water is drawn off by a small canal to irrigate the neighbouring land, and in a season of drought like this, very little of the abstracted part returns. They told me that the Moselle river never has been so "basse" for 30 years, and I was therefore an unlucky *voyageur* in having to do for the first time what could have been done more easily in any other season.

As evening fell I reached the town of Chatel, and got the Rob Roy a quiet bed in the wash-house of the hotel. But five minutes had not elapsed before a string of visitors came for the daily inspection.

As I sauntered along the bridge a sprightly youth came up, who had not seen the canoe, but who knew I was "one of her crew." He was most enthusiastic on the subject, and took me to see *his* boat, a deadly-looking flat-bottomed open cot, painted all manner of patterns; and as he was extremely proud of her I did not tell him that I consider a boat is like a woman, too good to paint: a pretty one is spoiled by paint, and a plain one is made hideous.

Then he came for a look at the Rob Roy, and, poor fellow, it was amusing to observe how instantly his countenance fell from pride to intense envy. He had a "boating mind," but had never seen a really pretty boat till now. However, to console himself he invited me to another hotel to drink success to the canoe in Bavarian beer, and to see my drawings, and then I found my intelligent, eager, and, I may add, gentlemanly friend was the waiter there!

A melancholy sensation pervaded the Rob Roy to-day, in consequence of a sad event, the loss of the captain's knife. We had three knives on board in starting from England; one I had given away in reward for some signal service, and this which was now lost was one with a metal haft and a curious hook at the end, a special description made in Berlin, and very useful to the tourist. It is not to be wondered that in so many leaps and somersaults, and with such constant requirements for the knife to mend pencils, &c., &c., the trusty blade should at last have disappeared, but the event suggests to the next canoeman that his boat-knife should be secured to a lanyard.

One singular conformation of the river-bed occurred in my short tour upon this part of the Moselle. Without much warning the banks of rock became quite vertical and narrowed close together. They reminded me of the rock-cutting near Liverpool, on the old railway to Manchester. The stream was very deep here, but its bed was full of enormous stones and crags, very sharp and jagged, which, however, could be easily avoided, because the current was gentle.

A man I found fishing told me that a little farther on there was an "impossible" place, so when after half a mile I heard the well-known sound of rushing waters (the ear got marvellous quick for this), I beat to quarters and prepared for action.

The ribbon to keep my hat was tied down. Sleeves and trousers were tucked up. The covering was braced tight and the baggage secured below; and then came the eager pleasures of anticipating, wishing, hoping, fearing, that are mixed up in the word excitement.

The sound was quite near now, but the river took the strangest of all the forms I had yet seen.

If you suppose a trench cut along Oxford-street to get at the gas-pipes, and if all the water of a river which had filled the street before suddenly disappeared in the trench, that would be exactly what the Moselle had now become.

The plateau of rock on each side was perfectly dry, though in flood times, no doubt, the river covers that too. The water boiled and foamed through this channel from 3 to 20 feet deep, but only in the trench, which was not five feet wide.

An intelligent man came near to see me enter this curious passage, but when I had got a little way in I had to stop the boat, and this too by putting my hands on both sides of the river.

Then I got out and carefully let the boat drive along the current, while I held by the painter. Soon it got too narrow and fast even for this process, so I pulled the canoe upon the dry rock, and sat down to breathe and to cool my panting frame.

Two other gentlemen had come by this time, and on a bridge above were several more with two ladies.

I had to drag the boat some hundred yards over most awkward rocks, and these men hovered round and admired, and even talked to me, and praised my perseverance, yet not one offer of any help did any one of them give!

In deep water again, and now exactly under the bridge I looked up and found the whole party regarding the Rob Roy with curiosity and smiles. Within a few yards was a large house these people had come from, and I thought their smiles were surely to preface, "Would you not like a glass of wine, Sir, after your hour of hard work?" But as it meant nothing of the sort I could not help answering their united adieux! by these words, "Adieu, ladies and gentlemen. Many to look, but none to help. The exhibition is gratuitous!" Was I wrong to say this? It was utterly impossible not to think it.

One or two other places gave trouble without interest, such as when I had to push the boat into a hedge point foremost, and to pull it through by main force from the other side, and then found, after all, it was pushed into the wrong field, so the operation had to be done over again in a reverse direction.

But never mind, all this counted in the day's work, and all the trouble of it was forgotten after a good night's sleep, or entirely recompensed by some interesting adventure.

The water of the Moselle is so clear that the scenery under the surface continually occupied my attention. In one long reach, unusually deep and quiet, I happened to be gazing down at some huge trout, and I accidentally observed a large stone, the upper part of a fine column, at the very bottom of the water, at least ten feet below me. The capital showed it to be Ionic, and near it was another, a broken pediment of large dimensions, and a little farther on a pedestal of white marble. I carefully examined both banks, to see if a Roman villa or bridge, or other ruin, indicated how these subaqueous reliques had come into this strange position, and I inquired diligently at Charmes, the next town; but although much curiosity was shown on the matter, no information was obtained, except that the Romans had built a fort somewhere on the river (but plainly not at that spot), so I consider that the casual glance at the fish revealed a curious fragment of the past hitherto probably unnoticed.

After pulling along the Moselle, from as near to its source as my canoe could find water, until the scenery became dull at Charmes, we went by railway from thence to Blainville, on the river Meurthe, which is a tributary of the Moselle, for I thought some new scenery might be found in this direction. The Rob Roy was therefore sent by itself in a goods-train, the very first separation between us for three months. It seemed as if the little boat, leaning on its side in the truck, turned from me reproachfully, and I foreboded all sorts of accidents to its delicate frame, but the only thing lost was a sponge, a necessary appendage to a boat's outfit when you desire to keep it perfectly dry and clean. Two railway porters, with much good-humoured laughing, carried the Rob Roy from the station to the river's edge, and again I paddled cheerily along, and on a new river, too, with scenery and character quite different from that of the Moselle.

The Meurthe winds through rich plains of soft earth, with few rocks and little gravel. But then in its shallows it has long thick mossy weeds, all under the surface. I found these rather troublesome, because they got entangled with my paddle, and they could not be seen beforehand, and the channel was, therefore, not discernible as where rocks or gravel give those various forms of ripples which the captain of a canoe soon gets to know as if they were a chart telling the number of inches of depth. Moreover, when you get grounded among these long weeds, all pointed down stream, it is very difficult to "back out," for it is like combing hair against the grain.

The larger rivers in France are all thoroughly fished. In every nook you find a fisherman. They are just as numerous here as in Germany they are rare. And yet one would think that fishing is surely more adapted to the contemplative German than to the vivacious French. Yet, here they are by hundreds, both men and women, and

"French Fishers."

every day, each staring intensely on a tiny float, or at the grasshopper bait, and quite content now and then to pull up a gudgeon the size of your thumb.

Generally, these people are alone, and when they asked me at hotels if I did not feel lonely in the canoe, I said, "Look at your fishermen, for hours by choice alone. They have something to occupy attention every moment, and so have I."

Sometimes, however, there is a whole party in one clumsy boat.

The *pater familias* sits content, and recks not if all his time is spent in baiting his line and lighting his pipe. The lazy "hopeful" lies at full length on the grass, while a younger brother strains every nerve to hook a knowing fish that is laughing at him under water, and winking its pale eye to see the fisher just toppling over. Mademoiselle chatters whether there are bites or not, and another, the fair cousin, has got on shore, where she can bait her hook and simper to the bold admirer by her side.

Not one of these that I have spoken to had ever seen an artificial fly.

Then besides, we have the fishers with nets. These are generally three men in a boat, with its stem and stern both cocked up, and the whole affair looking as if it must upset or sink. Such boats were painted by Raphael in the great cartoons, where all of us **must** have observed how small the boat is compared with the men it carries.

Again, there are some young lads searching under the stones for *ecrevisses*, the freshwater prawns, much in request, but giving very little food for a great deal of trouble. Near these fishers the pike plies his busy sportsman's life below the surface, and I have sometimes seen a poor little trout leap high into the air to escape from the long-nosed pursuer, who followed him even out of the water, and snapped his jaws impudently on the sweet morsel. This sound, added to the very suspicious appearance of the Rob Roy gliding among the islands, decides the doubtful point with a duck, the leader of a flock of wild ducks that have been swimming down stream in front of me with a quick glance on each side every moment, every one of them seemingly indignant at this intrusion on their haunts; at last, as if with one wing, they flap the water and rise in a body to seek if there be not at least some one nook elsewhere to nestle in where John Bull does not come.

That bell tinkling is at the ferry, to call the ferryman who lives at the other side, and he will jump into his clumsy boat, which is tied to a pulley running on a rope stretched tight across the river. He has only to put his oar obliquely on the gunwale, and the transverse effect of the current brings the boat rapidly to the other bank.

Paddling on, after a chat with the ferryman (and he is sure to be ready for that), a wonderful phenomenon appears. I see a house, large, new, and of two stories high, has actually moved.

I noticed it a few minutes ago, and now it has changed its position. I gaze in astonishment, and while I ponder, the whole house entirely disappears. Now, the true explanation of this is soon found when we get round the next corner of the reach;—the house is a great wooden bathing "etablissement," built on a barge, and it is being slowly dragged up the stream.

I noticed three women on the river-bank evidently in great alarm: it was a mother, a daughter, and a maid, who searched in vain for two boys, supposed to have gone away to fish, but now missing for many hours. They eagerly inquired if I had seen the lads, and implored me with tears to give them advice.

I tried all I could to recollect, but no! I had not seen the boys, and so the women went away distracted, and I was sorrowful—who would not be so at a woman's tears, and a mother's too? Suddenly, when toiling in the middle of a very difficult piece of rock-work, lowering the boat, I remembered having seen those boys, so I ran after the anxious mamma and convinced her the children had been safe an hour ago, and their faithful servant with them, but that *he* had become the fisherman, and they, like boys, had got tired of the rod, and were playing with a goat.

When I told the poor mother I had seen the little fellows and they were safe, her tears of joy were quite affecting, and vividly recalled one's schoolboy days, when the thoughtless play-time of childhood so often entails anxiety on a loving mother's heart.

Such, then, are the river sights and river wonders, ever new, though trifling, perhaps, when told, but far more lively and entertaining than the incidents of a dusty road, or a whirring, shrieking train.

With a few wadings and bumpings, and one or two "vannes," or weirs, I got on pleasantly until evening came on, and still the towers of St. Nicholas, visible on the horizon, seemed ever to move from side to side without being any nearer, so much does this river wind in its course. I paddled at my best pace, but the evening rapidly grew darker, until we overtook two French youths in a boat, the first occasion on which I had noticed Frenchmen rowing for exercise. They could not keep up with the canoe, so I had to leave them ingloriously aground on a bank, and yet too lazy to get out and help their boat over the difficulty.

Soon after I came to a great weir about fifteen feet in height, the deepest we had encountered, and it was a matter of some little trouble to get the boat over this in the dark; but what was far worse immediately followed, as I found myself in a maze of shallows, without light to see how to get out. Finally, I had to wade and haul the boat along, and jump in and ferry myself over the pools, for fully half a mile, until I was delighted to find a bridge and a house.

All this, which may be told in a few sentences, took a full hour of very tiresome work, though, as there was no current, there was no danger, and it was merely tedious, wet, and uncomfortable. When I came to the bridge, I was sure it must be a town, and then there happened a scene almost an exact counterpart of that which took place at Gegglingen, on the Danube.

I pulled up my boat on the dark shore, and, all dripping wet, I mounted to the house above, and speedily aroused the inmates. A window opened, and a worthy couple appeared in their night-dresses, holding a candle to examine the intruder. The tableau was most comical. The man asked, "Is it a farce?" He could scarcely expect a traveller from England to arrive there at such an hour. But he soon helped me to carry the boat to a little restaurant, where a dozen men were drinking, who rushed out with lamps to look at the boat, but entirely omitted to help the forlorn captain.

Nor was there any room in this restaurant, so we had to carry the boat through the dark streets to another house, where another lot of topers received me in like style. I put the Rob Roy into a garden here, and her sails flapped next morning while a crowd gazed over the walls with anxious curiosity. The worthy husband who had thus left his spouse that he might carry **my** wet boat, all slippery with mud, was **highly** pleased **with** a five-franc piece, which was the least I thought him to deserve, though it was like a five-pound note to him in such a cheap country.

Next morning in the light of day I had a survey of the scene of last night's adventure. It was very amusing to trace the various channels I had groped about in the darkness.

Here I met a French gentleman, of gay and pleasant manner, but who bemoaned his lot as Secretary of a great factory in this outlandish place, instead of being in joyous, thoughtless, brilliant Paris, where, he said, often for days together he did not sleep in bed, but ran one night into the next by balls, theatres, and supper parties.

He kindly took me to see the great salt works, that send refined salt all over Europe. This rock salt is hoisted out of a deep mine, in blocks like those of coal, having been hewn from the strata below, which are pierced by long and lofty galleries. Then it is covered in tanks by water, which becomes saturated, and is conducted to flat evaporating pans, when the water is expelled by the heat of great furnaces, and the salt appears in masses like snow-drifts. Salt that is sold by weight they judiciously wet again, and other qualities sold by measure they cleverly cause to deposit itself in crooked crystals, so as to take up as much space as possible!

We found a canal here, and as the river was so shallow I mounted to the artificial channel, and with a strong and fair wind was soon sailing along rapidly. This canal has plenty of traffic upon it, and only a few locks; so it was by no means tedious. They asked for my card of permission, but I smiled the matter off as before. However, an officer of the canal who was walking alongside looked much more seriously at the infringement of rules, and when we came to a lock he insisted I must produce the "carte." As a last resort, I showed him the well-worn sketch-book, and then he at once gave in. In fact, after he had laughed at the culprit's caricatures, how could he gravely sentence him to penalties?

It is wonderful how a few lines of drawing will please these outlying country people. Sometimes I gave a small sketch to a man when it was desirable to get rid of him: he was sure to take it away to show outside, and when he returned I had departed. Once I gave a little girl a portrait of her brother, and next morning she brought it again all crumpled up. Her mother said the child had held it all night in her hand.

CHAPTER XIV.

Ladies in muslin—Officers shouting—Volunteers' umbrella—Reims—Leaks—Wet—Madame Clicquot—Heavy blow—Dinner talk—The Elephant—Cloud.

THE canal brought me to Nancy, a fine old town, with an archbishop, a field-marshal, a good hotel, large washhand basins, drums, bugles, ices, and all the other luxuries of life! In the cathedral there was more tawdry show about the Mass than I ever remarked before, even in Italy. At least thirty celebrants acted in the performance, and the bowings and turnings and grimaces of sedate old men clad in gorgeous, dirty needlework, fumbling with trifles and muttering Latin, really passed all bounds: they were an insult to the population, who are required to attend this vicarious worship, and to accept such absurdities as the true interpretation of " This do in remembrance of me." A large and attentive congregation, nearly all women, listened first to an eloquent sermon from a young priest who glorified an old saint. It is possible that the ancient worthy was a most respectable monk, but probably he was, when he lived, a good deal like the monks one meets in the monasteries, and now that I have lived pretty frequently with these gentlemen I must say it makes one smile to think of canonizing such people, as if any one of them had unapproachable excellence; but perhaps this monk distinguished himself by proper daily ablutions, and so earned the rare reputation of being reasonably clean. In the afternoon the relics of the monk were borne through the streets by a procession of some thousand women and a few men. These ladies, some hundreds of whom were dressed in white muslin, and in two single ranks, chanted as they slowly marched, and all the bystanders took off their hats, but I really could not see what adoration was due to the mouldering bones of a withered friar, so my excellent straw hat was kept on my head.

But the French, who live in public, must have a public religion, a gregarious worship, with demonstrative action and colours and sounds. Deep devotion, silent in its depth, is for the north and not for this radiant sun, though you will find that quiet worship again in lower latitudes where the very heat precludes activity.

Some twenty years ago, one of the ablest men of the University of Cambridge read a paper on the influence which the insular position and the climate of Britain has upon our national character, and it appeared to be proved clearly that this influence pervades every feature of our life.

In a third-rate French town like Nancy, nearly all the pleasant *agrements* depend on the climate, and would be sadly curtailed by rain or snow. So, again, when a Frenchman visits England and gets laughed at for mistakes in our difficult language, and has to eat only two dishes for dinner, and drinks bad coffee, and has no evening lounge in the open air, and is then told to look at our domestic life, and finds he cannot get an entrance there (for how very few French do enter there), his miseries are directly caused by our climate, and no wonder his impression of Albion is that we are all fog and cotton and smoke, and everything *triste*.

From Nancy I sent the canoe by rail to meet me on the river Marne, and while the slow luggage-train lumbered along I took the opportunity of visiting the celebrated Camp of Châlons, the Aldershot of France. An omnibus takes you from the railway station, and you soon enter a long straggling street of very little houses, built badly, and looking as if one and all could be pushed down by your hand. These are not the military quarters, but the self-grown parasite sutlers' town, which springs up near every camp.

Here is "Place Solferino," and there "Rue Malakhoff," where the sign of the inn is a Chinaman having his pigtail lopped off by a Français. The camp is in the middle of a very large plain, with plenty of dust and white earth, which "glared" on my eyes intensely, this being the hottest day I have experienced during the vacation. But there are trees for shade, and a good deal of grass on the extensive downs where great armies can manœuvre and march past the Emperor as he sits enthroned under a bower on that hill-crest overlooking all.

The permanent buildings for the troops consist of about 500 separate houses, substantial, airy, and well lighted, all built of brick, and slated, and kept in good repair; each of these is about seventy feet long, twenty broad, and of one story high. About a million and a-half pounds sterling have already been expended on this camp. Behind the quarters are the soldiers' gardens, a feature added lately to the camps in England. There were only a few thousand soldiers at the place, so I soon saw everything interesting, and then adjourned to a restaurant, where I observed about twenty officers go in a body to breakfast. This they did in a separate room, but their loud, coarse, and outrageously violent conversation really amazed me. The din was monstrous and without intermission. I had never before fallen in with so very bad a specimen of French manners, and I cannot help thinking there may have been special reasons for these men bellowing for half an hour as they ate their breakfast.

The "mess system" has been tried in the French army several times, but it seems to fail always, as the French Clubs do, on the whole. It is not wise, however, for a traveller to generalize too rapidly upon the character of any portion of a great people if he has not lived long among them. A hasty glance may discern that a stranger has a long nose, but you must have better acquaintance with him before you can truly describe the character of your friend. In a little book just published in France about the English Bar two facts are noted, that Barristers put the name of their "inn" on their visiting cards, and that the Temple Volunteers are drilled admirably by a Serjeant-at-Law, who wields "an umbrella with a varnished cover, which glances in the sun like a sword."

Another interesting town in this department of France is Rheims (spelt Reims, and pronounced very nearly Rens). Having still an hour or two free, I went there, and enjoyed the visit to the very splendid cathedral. It is one of the finest in Europe, very old, very large, very rich, and celebrated as the place of coronation for the French sovereigns. Besides all this it is kept in good order, and is remarkably clean. The outside is covered with stone figures, most of them rude in art, but giving at a distance an appearance of prodigal richness of material. A little periodical called *France Illustrated* is published at fourpence each number, with a map of the Department, several woodcuts of notable places or events, and a brief history of the principal towns, concluding with a *résumé* of the statistics of the Department. A publication of this kind would, I think, be very useful in England; and for travellers especially, who could purchase at the county town the particular number or part then required.

In one of the adjoining Departments, according to this publication, it appears that there are about a hundred suicides in the year among a population of half a million. Surely this is an alarming proportion; and what should we say if Manchester had to report 100 men and women in one year who put themselves to death?

But we are subsiding, you see, into the ordinary tales of a traveller, because I am waiting now for the train and the Rob Roy, and certainly this my only experience of widowerhood made me long again for the well-known yellow oaken side of the boat and her pink-brown cedar varnished top.

Well, next morning here is the canoe at Epernay, arrived all safe at a cost of 2s. 6d. All safe, I thought at first, but I soon found it had been sadly bruised, and would surely leak. I turned it upside down on the railway platform, and bought two candles and occupied three good hours in making repairs and greasing all the seams. But after all this trouble, when I put the boat into the Marne, the water oozed in all round.

It is humiliating to sit in a leaky boat—it is like a lame horse or a crooked gun; and of all the needful qualities of a boat the first is to keep out the water. So I stopped at the first village, and got a man to mix white lead and other things, and we carefully worked this into all the seams, leaving it to harden while I had my breakfast in the little auberge close by the shore, where they are making the long rafts to go down to Paris, and where hot farmers come to sip their twopenny bottle of wine.

The raft man was wonderfully proud of his performance with the canoe, and he called out to each of his friends as they walked past, to give them its long history in short words. When I paid him at last, he said he hoped I would never forget that the canoe had been thoroughly mended in the middle of France, at the village of ——, but I really do not remember the name.

However, there were not wanting tests of his workmanship, for the Rob Roy had to be pulled over many dykes and barriers on the Marne. Some of these were of a peculiar construction, and were evidently novel in design.

A "barrage" reached across the stream, and there were three steps or falls on it, with a plateau between each. The water ran over these steps, and was sometimes only a few inches in depth on the crest of each fall, where it had to descend some eight or ten inches at most.

This, of course, would have been easy enough for the canoe to pass, but then a line of iron posts was ranged along each plateau, and chains were tied from the top of one post to the bottom of another, diagonally, and it will be understood that this was a very puzzling arrangement to steer through.

In cases of this sort I usually got ashore to reconnoitre, and, having calculated the angle at which I must enter the passage obliquely, down a fall, and across its stream, I managed to get successfully through several of these strange barriers. We came at length to one which, on examination, I had to acknowledge was "impassable," for the

"The Chain Barrier."

chains were slack, and there was only an inch or two of "law" on either side of the difficult course through them.

However, a man happened to see my movements and the canoe, and soon he called some dozen of his fellow navvies from their work to look at the navigator.

I was therefore incited by these spectators to try the passage, and I mentally resolved at any rate to be cool and placid, however much discomfiture was to be endured. I steered to the very best of my power, but the bow of the canoe swerved an inch in the swift oblique descent, and instantly it got locked in the chains, while I quietly got out (whistling an air in slow time), and then, in the water with all my clothes on, I steadily lifted the boat through the iron network and got into her, dripping wet, but trying to behave as if it were only the usual thing. The navvies cheered a long and loud bravo! but I felt somewhat ashamed of having yielded to the desire for ignorant applause, and when finally round the next corner I got out and changed my wet things, a wiser and a sadder man, but dry.

This part of the river is in the heart of the champagne country, and all the softly swelling hills about are thickly covered by vineyards. The vine for champagne is exceedingly small, and grows round one stick, and the hillside looks just like a carding-brush, from the millions of these little sharp-pointed rods upright in the ground and close together, without any fence whatever between the innumerable lots. The grape for champagne is always red, and never white, so they said, though white grapes are grown for "eating." During the last two months few people have consumed more grapes in this manner than the chief mate of the Rob Roy canoe.

On one of these hills I noticed the house of Madame Clicquot, whose name has graced many a cork of champagne bottles (and of bottles not champagne). The vineyards of Ai, near Epernay, are the most celebrated for their wine. After the bottles are filled, they are placed neck downwards, and the sediment collects near the cork. Each bottle is then uncorked in this position, and the confined gas forces out a little of the wine with the sediment, while a skilful man dexterously replaces the cork when this sediment has been expelled. I should say that only a very skilful man can perform such a feat. When the bottles are stored in "caves," or vast cellars, the least change of temperature causes them to burst by hundreds. Sometimes one-fourth of the bottles explode in this manner, and it is said that the renowned Madame Clicquot lost 400,000 in the hot autumn of 1843 before sufficient ice could be fetched from Paris to cool her spacious cellars. Every year about fifty million bottles of genuine champagne are made in France, and no one can say how many more millions of bottles of champagne are imbibed every year by a confiding world.

The Marne is a large and deep river, and its waters are kept up by barriers every few miles. It is rather troublesome to pass these (by taking the boat out and letting it down on the other side), and in crossing one of them I gave a serious blow to the stern of the canoe against an iron bar.

This blow started four planks from the sternpost, and revealed to me also that the whole frame had suffered from the journey at night on an open truck. However, as my own ship's carpenter was on board, and had nails and screws, I soon managed to make all tight again, and by moonlight found myself at Dormans, where I got two men to carry the boat as usual to an hotel, and had the invariable run of visitors from that time until everybody went to bed.

It is curious to remark the different names by which the canoe has been called, and among these the following:—"*Batteau,*" "*schiff,*" "*bôt,*" "*barca,*" "*canôt,*" "*caique*" (the soldiers who have been in the Crimea call it thus), "*chaloupe,*" "*navire,*" "*schipp*" (Low German), "*yacht*" ("jacht"—Danish, "jaht," from "jagen," to ride quickly—properly a boat drawn by horses). Several people have spoken of it as "*batteau à vapeur,*" for in the centre of France they have never seen a steamboat, but the usual name with the common people is "*petit batteau,*" and among the educated people "*nacelle*" or "*perissoir;*" this last as we call a dangerous boat a "coffin" or "sudden death."

An early start next morning found me slipping along with a tolerable current and a fine fresh breeze, but the same unalterable blue sky. I had several interesting conversations with farmers and others riding to market along the road which here skirts the river. What most surprises the Frenchman is that a traveller can possibly be happy alone! Not one hour have I had of *ennui*, and, however selfish it may seem, I must aver that for this sort of journey I very much prefer to travel entirely *seul*.

Pleasant trees, wild fowl, and pretty gardens are all along in plenty, but where are the houses of the gentlemen of France, and where are the French gentlemen themselves? Here is a difference between France and England which cannot fail to "knock" the observant traveller (as Artemus Ward would say)—the notable absence of country seats during hours and hours of passage along the best routes; whereas in England the prospect from almost every hill of woodland would have a great house at the end of its vista, and the environs of every town would stretch into outworks of villas smiling in the sun. The French have ways and fashions which are not ours, but their nation is large enough to entitle them to a standard of their own, just as the Americans, with so great a people agreed on the matter, have surely liberty to speak with a nasal twang, and to spell "plough" without a "g."

I am convinced that it is a mistake to say we

are a silent people compared with the French or Americans. At some hundred sittings of the table d'hôte in both these countries I have found more of dull, dead silence than in England at our inns. An Englishman accustomed to the pleasant chat of a domestic dinner feels ill at ease when dining with strangers, and so notices their silence all the more; but the French table d'hôte (not in the big barrack hotels, for English tourists, I have before remarked upon) has as little general conversation, and an American one has far less than in England. Here come six or seven middle-class men to dine. They put the napkin kept for each from yesterday, and recognized by the knot they tied on it, up to their chins like the pinafore of a baby, and wipe plate, fork, and spoons with the other end, and eat bits and scraps of many dishes, and scrape their plates almost clean, and then depart, and not one word has been uttered.

Then, again, there is the vaunted French climate. Bright sun, no doubt, but forget not that it is so very bright as to compel all rooms to be darkened from ten to four each day. At noon the town is like a cemetery; no one thinks of walking, riding, or looking out of his window in the heat. From seven to nine in the morning, and from an hour before sunset to any time you please at night, the open air is delicious. But I venture to say that in a week of common summer weather we see more of the sun in England than in France, for we seldom have so much of it at once as to compel us to close our eyes against its fierce rays. In fact, the sensation of life in the South, after eleven o'clock in the morning, is that of waiting for the cool hours, and so day after day is a continual reaching forward to something about to come; whereas, an English day of sunshine is an enjoyable present from beginning to end. Once more, let it be remembered that twilight lasts only for half an hour in the sunny South; that delicious season is a characteristic of the northern latitudes which very few Southerners have ever experienced at all.

The run down the Marne for about 200 miles was a pleasant part of the voyage, but seldom so exciting in adventure as the paddling on unknown waters. Long days of work could therefore be now well endured, for constant exercise had trained the body, and a sort of instinct was enough, when thus educated by experience, to direct the mind. Therefore, the Rob Roy's paddle was in my hands for ten hours at a time without weariness, and sometimes even for twelve hours at a stretch.

After a comfortable night at Chateau Thierry

in the Elephant Hotel, which is close to the water, I took my canoe down from the hayloft to which it had been hoisted, and once more launched her on the river. The current gradually increased, and the vineyards gave place to forest trees. See, there are the rafts, some of casks, lashed together with osiers, some of planks, others of hewn logs, and others of great rough trees. There is a straw hut on them for the captain's cabin, and the crew will have a stiff fortnight's work to drag, push, and steer this congeries of wood down to the Seine. The labour spent merely in adjusting and securing the parts is enormous, but labour of that kind costs little here.

Farther on there is a large flock of sheep conducted to the river to drink, but (be it known) also driven to the water by the sagacious shepherds' dogs, who seem to know perfectly that the woolly multitude has come precisely to drink, and, therefore, the dogs cleverly press forward each particular sheep, until it has got a place by the cool brink of the water. In the next quiet bay a village maid drives her cow to the river, and chats across the water with another, also leading a cow to wade in knee deep, and to dip its broad nose, and lift it gently again from the cool stream. On the road alongside is a funny little waggon, and a whole family are within. This concern is actually drawn along by a goat. Its little kid skips about, for the time of toil has not yet come to the youngling, and it may gambol now. But here is the bridge of Nogent, so I leave my boat in charge of an old man, and give positive pleasure to the cook at the auberge by ordering a breakfast. Saints' portraits adorn the walls, and a "sampler" worked by some little girl, with only twenty-five letters in the alphabet, for the " w " is as yet ignored in classic grammars, though it has now to be constantly used in the common books and newspapers. Why, they even adopt our sporting terms, and you see in a paper that such a race was only " un Walkover," and that another was likely to be " un dead heat."

Suddenly the sky was shaded, and on looking up amazed I found a cloud; at last, after six weeks of brilliant blue and scorching glare, one fold of the fleecy curtain has been drawn over the sun.

The immediate effect of this cooler sky was very invigorating, though, after weeks of hot glare (reflected upwards again into the face from the water), it seemed the most natural thing to be always in a blaze of light, and much of the inconvenience was avoided by a plan which will be found explained in the Appendix, with some other hints to " Boating Men."

The day went pleasantly now, and with only the events of ordinary times, which need not be recounted. The stream was steady, the banks were peopled, and many a blue-bloused countryman stopped to look at the canoe as she glided past, with the captain's socks and canvas shoes on the deck behind him, for this was his drying-place for wet clothes.

Now and then a pleasure-boat was seen, and there were several canoes at some of the towns, but all of them flat-bottomed and open, and desperately unsafe—well named " perissoirs." Some of these were made of metal. The use of this is well known to be a great mistake for any boat under ten tons; in all such cases it is much heavier than wood of the same strength, considering the strains which a boat must expect to undergo.

" La Ferté sous Jouarre " is the long name of the next stopping-place. There are several towns called by the name La Ferté (La Fortifié), which in some measure corresponds with the termination "caster" or "cester" of English names. Millstones are the great specialty of this La Ferté. A good millstone costs 50*l*., and there is a large exportation of them. The material has

T

the very convenient property of not requiring to be chipped into holes, as these exist in this stone naturally.

At La Ferté I put the boat into a hayloft: how often it has occupied this elevated lodgings amongst its various adventures; and at dinner with me there is an intelligent and hungry bourgeois from Paris, with his vulgar and hearty wife, and the gossip of the town, who kept rattling on the stupid, endless fiddle-faddle of everybody's doings, sayings, failings, and earnings. Some amusement, however, resulted from the collision of two gossips at our table of four guests, for while the one always harped upon family tales of La Ferté and the minute sayings of its people, the other kept struggling to turn our thoughts to shoes and slippers, for he was a commercial traveller with a cartful of boots to sell. But, after all, how much of our conversation in better life is only of the same kind, though about larger, or at any rate different things; what might sound trifles to our British Cabinet would be the loftiest politics of Honolulu.

When we started at eight o'clock next day I felt an unaccountable languor; my arms were tired, and my energy seemed, for the first time, deficient. This was the result of a week's hard exercise, and of a sudden change of wind to the south. Give me our English climate for real hard work to prosper in.

One generally associates the north wind with cool and bracing air, and certainly in the Mediterranean it is the change of wind to the south, the hated *sirocce*, which enervates the traveller at once. But this north wind on the Marne came over a vast plain of arid land heated by two months of scorching sun, whereas the breezes of last week, though from the east, had been tempered in passing over the mountains of the Vosges.

Forty-two miles lay before me to be accomplished before arriving to-night at my resting-place for Sunday, and it was not a pleasant prospect to contemplate with stiff muscles in the shoulders. However, after twelve miles I found I could cut off about twenty miles in turnings of the river by putting the boat on a cart, and thus a league of walking and 3s. 4d. of payment solved the difficulty. The old man with his cart was interesting to talk to, and we spoke about those deep subjects which are of common interest to all.

At a turn in the road we came upon a cart overturned and with a little crowd round it, while the earth was covered with a great pool of what seemed to be blood, but was only wine. The cart had struck a tree, and the wine-cask on it instantly burst, which so frightened the horse that he overset the cart.

The Rob Roy was soon in the water again, and the scenery had now become much more enjoyable.

I found an old soldier at a ferry who fetched me a bottle of wine, and then he and his wife sat in their boat and became very great friends with the Englishman.

He had been at the taking of Constantine in Algeria, a place which really does look quite impossible to be taken by storm. But the appearance of a fortress is deceptive except to the learned in such matters. Who would think that Comorn, in Hungary, is stronger than Constantine? When you get near Comorn there is nothing to see, and it is precisely because of this that it was able to resist so long.

The breeze soon freshened till I hoisted my sails and was fairly wafted on to Meaux, so that, after all, the day, begun with forebodings, became as easy and as pleasant as the rest.

CHAPTER XV.

Hammering—Popish forms—Wise dogs—Blocked up—No water—Odd fellows—Dream on the Seine—Charing-cross.

THERE are three hemispheres of scenery visible to the traveller who voyages thus in a boat on the rivers. First, the great arch of sky, and land, and trees, and flowers down to the water's brink; then the whole of this reflected beautifully in the surface of the river; and then the wondrous depths in the water itself, with its animal life, its rocks and glades, and its flowers and mosses. Now rises the moon so clear, and with the sky around it so black that no "man in the moon" can be seen.

At the hotel we find a whole party of guests for the marriage-dinner of a newly-wedded pair. The younger portion of the company adjourn to the garden and let off squibs and crackers, so it seems to be a good time to exhibit some of my signal lights from my bedroom-window, and there is much cheering at the Englishman burning magnesium wire, which illumines the whole neighbourhood like the electric light. Next day the same people all assembled for a marriage breakfast, and sherry, madeira, and champagne flowed from the well-squeezed purse of the bride's happy father.

I have noticed that the last sound to give way to the stillness of the night in a village is that of the blacksmith's hammer, which is much more heard abroad than at home. Perhaps this is because much of their execrable French ironwork is made in each town; whereas in England it is manufactured by machinery in great quantities and at special places. At any rate, one associates with the Continent (after travelling long enough to have got calm and observant, seeing, hearing, and, we may add, scenting all around) blue dresses, white stones, jingling of bells, and the "cling, cling" of the never idle blacksmith.

This town of Meaux has a bridge with houses on it, and great mill-wheels filling up the arches as they used to do in old London-bridge. Pleasant gardens front the river, and cafés glitter there at night. These are not luxuries but positive necessaries of life for the Frenchman, and it is their absence abroad which—I believe—is one chief cause of his being so bad a colonist, for the Frenchman has only the expression "with me" for "home," and no word for "wife" but "woman."

The cathedral of Meaux is grand and old, and

see how they masquerade the service in it! Look at the gaunt "Suisse," with his cocked-hat kept on in church, and his sword and spear. The twenty priests and twelve red-surpliced boys intone to about as many hearers. A monk escorted through the church makes believe to sprinkle holy water on all sides from that dirty plasterer's brush, and then two boys carry on their shoulders a huge round loaf, the "pain benit," which, after fifty bowings, is blessed, and escorted back to be cut up, and is then given in morsels to the congregation. These endless ceremonies are the meshes of the net of Popery, and they are well woven to catch Frenchmen, who must have action, show, the visible tangible outside, whatever may be meant by it.

This service sets one a-thinking. Some form there must be in worship. One can suppose, indeed, that perfect spirit can adore God without attitude, or even any sequence or change. Yet in the Bible we hear of seraphs veiling their bodies with their wings, and of elders prostrate at certain times, and saints that have a litany even in heaven. Mortals must have some form of adoration, but there is the question, How much? and on this great point how many wise and foolish men have written books without end, or scarcely any effect!

The riverside was a good place for a quiet Sunday walk. Here a flock of 300 sheep had come to drink, and nibble at the flowers hanging over the water, and the simple-hearted shepherd stood looking on while his dogs rushed backward and forward, yearning for some sheep to do wrong, that their dog service might be required to prevent or to punish naughty conduct. This "Berger" inquired whether England was near Africa, and how large our legs of mutton are, and if we have sheep-dogs, and are there any rivers in our island on the sea. Meanwhile at the hotel the marriage party kept on "breakfasting," even until four o'clock, and non-melodious songs were sung. The French, as a people, do not excel in vocal music, either in their tones or their harmonies.

Afloat again next morning, and quite refreshed, I prepared for a long day's work. The stream was now clear, and the waving tresses of dark green weeds gracefully curved under water, while islands amid deep shady bays varied the landscape above.

I saw a canal lock open, and paddled in merely for variety, passing soon into a tunnel, in the middle of which I found a huge boat fixed, and nobody with it. The boat exactly filled the tunnel, and the men had gone to their dinner, so I had to drag the boat out, and then the canoe proudly glided into daylight, having a whole tunnel to itself.

At Lagny, where I wished to breakfast, I left my boat with a nice old gentleman, who was fishing in a nightcap and spectacles, and he assured me he would stop there two hours. But when I scrambled back through the mill (the miller's men amazed among their wholesome dusty sacks), I found the boat all alone, the first time she had been left in a town an "unprotected female."

To escape a long serpent wind of the river, I entered another canal and found it about a foot deep, with clear water flowing pleasantly. This I thought was very fortunate for me, and it was enjoyed most thoroughly for a few miles, little knowing what was to come. Presently weeds began, then clumps of great rushes, then large bushes and trees, all growing with thick grass in the water, and at length this got so dense that the prospect before me was precisely like a very large hayfield, with grass four feet high, all ready to be mowed, but which had to be mercilessly rowed through.

This on a hot day without wind, and in a long vista, unbroken by a man or a house, or anything lively, was rather daunting, but I had gone too far to recede with honour, and so by dint of pushing and working I actually got the boat through

"Canal Miseries."

some miles of this novel obstruction (known only this summer), and brought her safe and sound again to the river. At one place there was a bridge over this wet marsh, and two men happened to be going over it as the canoe came near. They soon called to some neighbours, and the row of spectators exhibited the faculty so notable in French people and so rarely found with us, that of being able to keep from laughing right out at a foreigner in an awkward case. The absurd sight of a man paddling a boat amid miles of thick rushes was indeed a severe test of courteous gravity.

However, I must say that the labour required to penetrate this marsh was far less than one would suppose from the appearance of the place. The sharp point of the boat entered, and its smooth sides followed through hedges, as it were, of aquatic plants, and, on the whole (and after all was done!), I preferred the trouble and muscular effort required then to that of the monotonous calm of usual canal sailing.

Fairly in the broad river again I found myself at Neuilly, and it was plain that my Sunday rest had enabled over thirty miles to be accomplished without any fatigue at the end. With some difficulty I selected an inn on the waterside. The canoe was taken up to it and put on a table in a summer-house, while my own bed was in a garret where I could not stand upright—the only occasion where I have been badly housed; and pray let no one be misled by the name of this abode—" The Jolly Rowers."

Next day the river flowed fast again, and numerous islands made the channels difficult to find. The worst of these difficulties is that you cannot prepare for them. No map gives any just idea of your route—the people on the river itself are profoundly ignorant of its navigation. For instance, in starting, my landlord told me that in two hours I should reach Paris. After ten miles an intelligent man said, "Distance from Paris! it is six hours from here;" while a third informed me a little farther on, "It is just three leagues and a half from this spot." The banks were now dotted with villas, and numerous pleasure-boats were moored at neat little stairs. The vast number of these boats quite astonished me, and the more so as very few of them were ever to be seen in actual use.

The French are certainly ingenious in their boat-making, but more of ingenuity than of practical exercise is seen on the water. In several rivers I remarked the "walking machine," by which a man can walk on the water by fixing two small boats on his feet. A curious mode of rowing has lately been invented by a Frenchman, a description of which will be found in the Appendix.

I stopped to breakfast at a new canal cutting, and as there were many *gamins* about, I fastened a stone to my painter and took the boat out into the middle of the river, and so left her moored within sight of the arbour, where I sat, and also within sight of the ardent-eyed boys who gazed for hours with wistful looks on the tiny craft and its little fluttering flag. Their desire to handle as well as to see is only natural for these little fellows, and, therefore, if the lads behave well, I always make a point of showing them the whole affair quite near, after they have had to abstain from it so long as forbidden.

Strange that this quick curiosity of French boys does not ripen some of them into travellers, but it soon gets expended in trifling details of a narrow circle, while the sober, sedate, nay, the triste, Anglian is found scurrying over the world with a carpet-bag, and pushing his way in foreign crowds without one word of their language, and all the while as merry as a lark. Among the odd modes of locomotion adopted by Englishmen, I have already mentioned that of the gentleman travelling in Germany with a four-in-hand and two spare horses. I met another Briton who had made a tour in a road locomotive which he bought for 700*l*., and sold again at the same price for India. Neither of these, however, could cross seas, lakes, and rivers like the canoe, which I could take wherever a man could walk or a plank could swim.

It seemed contrary to nature that, after thus nearing pretty Paris, one's back was now to be turned upon it for hours in order to have a wide, vague, purposeless voyage into country parts. But the river willed it so; for here a great curve began and led off to the left, while the traffic of the

Marne went straight through a canal to the right, —through a canal, and therefore I would not follow it there.

The river got less and less in volume; its water was used for the canal, and it could scarcely trickle, with its maimed strength, through a spacious sweep of real country life. Here I often got grounded, got entangled in long mossy weeds, got fastened in overhanging trees, and, in fact, suffered all the evils which the smallest brook had ever entailed, though this was a mighty river.

The bend was more and more inexplicable, as it turned more round and round, till my face was full in the sunlight at noon, and I saw that the course was now due south.

Rustics were there to look at me, and wondering herdsmen too, as if the boat was in mid Germany, instead of being close to Paris. Evidently boating men in that quarter never came here by the river, and the Rob Roy was a *rara avis* floating on a stream unused.

But the circle was rounded at last, as all circles are, however large they be; and we got back to the common route, to civilization, fishing men and fishing women, and on the broad Marne once more. So here I stopped a bit for a ponder.

And now we unmoor for the last time, and enter the Rob Roy for its final trip—the last few miles of the Marne, and of more than a thousand miles rowed and sailed since we started from England. I will not disguise my feeling of sadness then, and I wished that Paris was still another day distant.

For this journey in a canoe has been interesting, agreeable, and useful, though its incidents may not be realized by reading what has now been described. The sensation of novelty, freedom, health, and variety all day and every day was what cannot be recited. The close acquaintance with the people of strange lands, and the constant observation of nature around, and the unremitting attention necessary for progress, all combine to make a voyage of this sort improving to the mind thus kept alert, while the body thoroughly enjoys life when regular hard exercise in the open air dissipates the lethargy of these warmer climes.

These were my thoughts as I came to the Seine and found a cool bank to lie upon under the trees, with my boat gently rocking in the ripples of the stream below, and the nearer sound of a great city telling that Paris was at hand. "Here," said I, "and now is my last hour of life savage and free. Sunny days; alone, but not solitary; worked, but not weary"—as in a dream the things, places, and men I had seen floated before my eyes half closed. The panorama was wide, and fair to the mind's eye; but it had a tale always the same as it went quickly past—that vacation was over, and work must begin. Up, then, for this is not a life of mere enjoyment. Again into the harness of "polite society," the hat, the collar, the braces, the gloves, the waistcoat, the latch-key—perhaps, the razor—certainly the umbrella! How every joint and limb will rebel against these manacles, but they must be endured!

The gradual approach to Paris by gliding down the Seine was altogether a new sensation. By diligence, railway, or steamer, you have nothing like it—not certainly by walking into Paris along a dusty road.

For now I was smoothly carried on a wide and winding river, with nothing to do but to look and to listen while the splendid panorama majestically unfolds. Villas thicken, gardens get smaller as houses are closer, trees get fewer as walls increase. Barges line the banks, commerce and its movement, luxury and its adornments, spires and cupolas grow out of the dim horizon, and then bridges seem to float towards me, and the hum of life gets deeper and busier, while the pretty little tinkling sound of the river waters yields to the roar of traffic, and to that indescribable thrill which throbs in the air around this the capital of the Continent, the centre of the politics, the focus of the pleasure and splendour of the world.

In passing the island at Notre Dame I fortunately took the proper side, but even then I found a very awkward rush of water under the bridges. This was caused by the extreme lowness of the river, which on this very day was three feet lower than in the memory of man. The fall over each barrier, though wide enough, was so shallow that I saw at the last bridge the crowd above me evidently calculated upon my being upset; and they were nearly right too. The absence of other boats showed me (now experienced in such omens) that some great difficulty was at hand, but I also remarked that by far the greater number of observers had collected over one particular arch, where at first there seemed to be the very worst chance for getting through. By logical deduction I argued, "that must be the best arch, after all, for they evidently expect I will try it," and, with a horrid presentiment that my first upset was to be at my last bridge, I boldly dashed forward—whirl, whirl the waves, and grate, grate my iron keel; but I am through, and a rewarding Bravo! from the Frenchmen above is answered by a British "All right" from below

No town was so hard to find a place for the canoe in as the bright, gay Paris. I went to the floating baths; they would not have me. I paddled to the funny old ship; they shook their heads. I tried a coal wharf; but they were only civil there. Even the worthy washerwomen, my quondam friends, were altogether callous now about a harbour for the canoe.

In desperation I paddled to a bath which was getting repaired, but when my boat rounded the corner it was met by a volley of abuse from the proprietor for disturbing his fishing; he was just in the act of expecting the final bite of a *goujon*.

Relenting as I apologized and told the Rob Roy's tale, he housed her there for the night; and I shouldered my luggage and wended my way to an hotel.

Here is Meurice's, with the homeward tide of Britons from every alp and cave of Europe flowing through its salons. Here are the gay streets, too white to be looked at in the sun, and the penny *poupeé* theatres under the trees, and the dandies driving so stiff in hired carriages, and the dapper, little soldiers, and the gilded cafés.

Yes, it is Paris—and more brilliant than ever!

I faintly tried to hope, but—pray pardon me—utterly failed to believe that any person there had enjoyed his summer months with such excessive delight as the captain, the purser, the ship's cook, and cabin boy of the Rob Roy canoe.

Eight francs take the boat by rail to Calais. Two shillings take her thence to Dover. The railway takes her free to Charing Cross, and there two porters put her in the Thames again.

A flowing tide, on a sunny evening, bears her fast and cheerily straight to Searle's, there to debark the Rob Roy's cargo safe and sound and thankful, and to plant once more upon the shore of old England

> The flag that braved a thousand miles,
> The rapid and the snag.

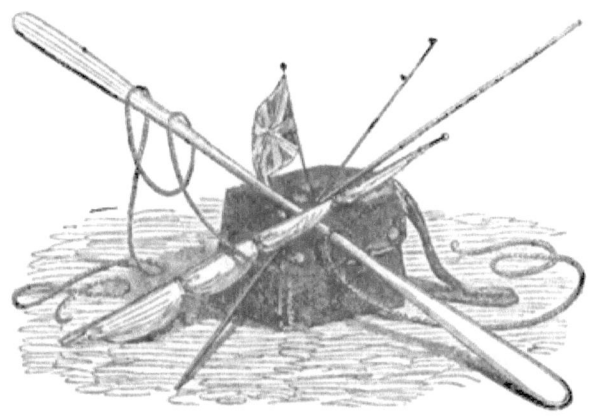

APPENDIX.

FOR CANOISTS.

THOSE who intend to make a river voyage on the Continent—and already several canoes are on the stocks for this purpose—will probably feel interested in some of the following information, while other readers of the foregoing pages may be indulgent enough to excuse the relation of a few particulars and technical details.

It is proposed, then, to give, first, a description of the canoe considered to be most suitable for a voyage of this sort after experience has aided in modifying the dimensions of the boat already used; second, an inventory of the cargo or luggage of the Rob Roy, with remarks on the subject, for the guidance of future passengers.

Next there will be found some notes upon currents in broken water; and lastly, some miscellaneous observations upon various points.

Although the Rob Roy and its luggage were not prepared until after much cogitation, it is well that intending canoists should have the benefit of what experience has since proved as to the faults and virtues of the arrangements devised for a first trip, after these have been thoroughly tasted in so pleasant a tour.

The best dimensions for the canoe appear to be—length, 13 feet; beam, 2 feet 2 inches; depth outside, from keel to deck, 9 inches; camber, 2 inches; keel, 1 inch, with a strip of iron, half an inch broad, carefully secured all the way below, and a copper strip up the stem and stern posts, and round the top of each of them. The opening in the deck should be 4 feet long (at most) and 20 inches wide, with a strong combing all round, but not more than 1 inch high. This opening should be semicircular at the ends, both for appearance sake and strength and convenience, so as to avoid corners. The macintosh sheet to cover this must be strong, to resist constant wear, light coloured, for the sun's heat, and so attached as to be readily loosened and made fast again, say 20 times a day. A water-tight compartment in the hull is a mistake. Its partition prevents access to breakages within, and arrests the circulation of air, and it cannot be kept long perfectly staunch. There should be extra timbers near the seat. The canoe must be so constructed as to endure without injury, (1) to be lifted by any part whatever; (2) to be rested on any part; (3) to be sat upon while aground, on any part of the deck, the combing, and the interior.

Wheels for transport have been often suggested, but they would be useless. On plain ground or grass you can readily do without them. On rocks and rough ground, or over ditches and through hedges,

APPENDIX. 295

wheels could not be employed, or would be in the way. Bilge pieces are not required. Strength must be had without them, and their projection seriously complicates the difficulties of pushing the boat over a pointed rock, both when afloat and when ashore.

The paddle should be 7 feet long (not more), strong, with both ends rounded, thick, and banded with copper. There should be conical cups to catch the dribbling water, and, if possible, some plan (not yet devised) for preventing or arresting the drops from the paddle ends, which fall on the deck when you paddle slowly, and when there is not enough centrifugal force to throw this water away from the boat. Painter of best flexible rope, not tarred, well able to bear 200lb. weight; more than 20 feet is a constant encumbrance. Ends secured through a hole in stem post and another in stern post (so that either or both can be readily cast off), the slack coiled on deck behind you.

There should be a back support of two wooden slips, each 15 inches by 3 inches, placed like the side strokes of the letter H, and an inch apart, but laced together with cord. Rest them against the edge of the combing, and so as to be free to yield to the motion of the back at each stroke, without hurting the spine. If made fast so as always to project, they are much in the way of the painter in critical times. They may be hinged below so as to fold down as you get out.

The mast should be 5 feet long, strong enough to stand gales without stays, stepped just forward of the stretcher, and so as to be struck without your rising when in a squall, or when nearing trees, or a bridge, barrier, ferry-rope, bank, or waterfall, or going aground.

The sail, if a lug, should have a fore leach of 4 feet, a head of 3 feet 6 inches, and a foot of 4 feet 6 inches; yard and boom of bamboo.

The boat can well stand more sail than this at sea, or in lakes and broad channels, but the foregoing size for a lug is quite large enough to manage in stiff breezes and in narrow rocky tortuous rivers.

A spritsail, on the whole, would be better as enabling more canvas to be carried, while it can be reduced at once to a leg of mutton sail by dropping the sprit in a gale.

The material of the sail should be strong cotton, in one piece, without any eyelet or hole whatever, but with a broad hem, enclosing well-stretched cord all round. A jib is of little use as a sail. It is apt to get aback in sudden turns. Besides, you must land to set it or to take in its outhaul, so as to be quite snug. But the jib does well to tie on the shoulders when they are turned to a fierce sun. The sails (with the booms or yards) should be rolled up round the mast compactly, to be stowed away forward, so that the end of the mast resting on the stretcher will keep the roll of sails out of the wet. The flag and its staff when not fast at the mast-head should fit into the mast-step, and should be light, so as not to sink if it falls overboard, as one of mine did.

The floor-boards should be strong, and easily detachable, so that one of them can be at once used as a paddle if that falls overboard.

APPENDIX. 297

The stretcher should have only one length, and let this be carefully determined after trial before starting. The two sides of its foot-board should be high and broad, while the middle may be cut down to let the hand get to the mast. The stretcher should, of course, be moveable, in order that you may lie down with the legs at full length for repose.

One brass cleat for belaying the halyard should be on deck, about the middle, and on the right-hand side. A stud on the other side, and this cleat will do to make one turn of the sheet round on either tack.

LIST OF STORES ON BOARD THE ROB ROY.

1. *Useful Stores.*—Paddle, painter (31 feet at first, but cut down to 20 feet), sponge, waterproof cover, 5 feet by 2 feet 3 inches, silk blue union jack, 10 inches by 8 inches, on a staff 2 feet long. Mast, boom, and yard. Lug sail, jib, and spare jib (used as a sun shawl). Stretcher, two back boards, floor boards, basket to sit on (12 inches by 6 inches, by 1 inch deep), and holding a macintosh coat. For repairs—iron and brass screws, sheet copper and copper nails, putty and whitelead, a gimlet, cord, string, and thread, a spare button, needle, and pins, canvas wading shoes (wooden clogs would be better); all the above should be left with the boat. Black bag for luggage, closed by three buttons, and with shoulder-strap, size, 12 inches by 12 inches, by 5 inches deep (just right). Flannel Norfolk jacket

(flaps not too long, else they dip in the water, or the pockets are inverted in getting out and in); wide flannel trousers, with broad back buckle, second trousers with belt (braces are better on shore). Flannel shirt on, and another for shore. **Thin alpaca** black Sunday coat, thick waistcoat, black leather **light-soled** spring-sided shoes (should be stronger for rocks **and** village pavements), straw hat, cloth cap (only used **as** a bag), 2 collars, 3 pocket handkerchiefs, ribbon tie, 2 pair of cotton socks (easily got **off for** sudden wading, and drying quickly **when** put **on deck in** the sun). Brush, comb, and tooth-brush. Testament, passport (scarcely needed after this winter), leather purse, circular notes, small change in silver and copper for frequent use, blue spectacles in strong case, book for journal and sketches, black, blue, and red chalk, and steel pen. Maps, cutting off a six inch square at a time for pocket reference. Pipe, **tobacco-case,** and light-box (metal, to resist moisture from without and within), guide books and pleasant evening reading book, you should cut off covers and all useless pages of these, and every page as read. **No** needless weight should be carried hundreds of miles; even a fly settling on the boat must be refused **a free** passage. Illustrated papers, tracts, and anecdotes in French and German for Sunday reading and daily distribution (far too few had been taken, they were always well received). Box of "Gregory's Mixture," sticking plaister, small **knife, and pencil.**

2. *Useless Articles.*—Boathook, undervest, waterproof helmet ventilated cap, foreign conversation books,

glass seltzer bottle and patent cork (for a drinking flask), tweezers for thorns.

3. *Lost or Stolen Articles.*—Bag for back cushion, waterproof bag for sitting cushion, long knife, necktie, woven waistcoat, box of quinine, steel-hafted knife. These, except the last of them, were not missed. I bought another thick waistcoat from a Jew.

ROCKS AND CURRENTS.

A few remarks may now be made upon the principal cases in which rocks and currents have to be dealt with by the canoist.

Even if rules could be laid down for the management of a boat in the difficult parts of a river, it would not be made easier until practice has given the boatman that quick judgment as to their application which has to be acquired in this and other athletic exercises, such as riding, skating, and even in walking.

It is only, therefore, as a subject of interest, and not by way of directions or instruction, that the following observations are here given; but the canoist who passes many hours every day for months together in the earnest consideration of the river problems always set before him for solution will probably feel some interest in this attempt to classify those that occur most frequently.

Steering a boat in a current among rocks is not unlike walking on a crowded pavement, where the other passengers are going in various directions, and at various speeds; and this operation of "threading your way" requires a great deal of practice, and not a few lessons learned in collisions, to make a pedestrian thoroughly *au fait* as a good man in a crowd. After years of walking through crowds, there is produced by an education of the mind and training of the body a certain power—not possessed by a novice—which insensibly directs a man in his course and his speed, but still his judgment has had to take cognizance of many varying *data* in the movements of other people which must have their effect upon each step he takes.

After this capacity becomes, as it were, instinctive, or, at any rate, acts almost involuntarily, a man can walk briskly along Fleet-street, and, without any distinct thought about other people, or about his own progress, he will safely get to his journey's end. Indeed, if he does begin to think of rules or how to apply them systematically, he is then almost sure to knock up against somebody else. Nay, if two men meet as they walk through a crowd, and each of them "catches the eye" of the other, they will probably cease to move instinctively, and, with uncertain data to reason from, a collision is often the result.

As the descent of a current among rocks resembles the walk along the pavement through a crowd, so the passage *across* a rapid is even more strictly in resemblance with the course of a man who has to cross a street where vehicles are passing at uncertain intervals and at various speeds, though all in the same direction. For it is plain that the thing to be done is nearly the same, whether the obstacles (as breakers) are fixed and the current carries you towards them, or the obstacles (as cabs and carts) are moving, while you have to walk through them on *terra firma*.

To cross Park-lane at four o'clock p.m. requires the very same sort of calculation as the passage across a rapid on the Rhine.

The importance of this subject will be considered sufficient to justify these remarks when the canoist has by much practice at last attained to that desirable proficiency which enables him to steer without thinking about it, and therefore to enjoy the conversation of others or the scenery on the bank, while he is rapidly speeding through rocks, eddies, and currents.

We may divide the rocks thus encountered into two classes—(1) Those that are *sunk*, so that the boat can perhaps float over them, and the direction of the current is not altered. (2) Those that are *breakers*, and so deflect the direction of the current, and do not allow the boat to float over them.

The currents may be divided into—(1) Those that are equable in force, and in the same direction through the course to be steered. (2) Those that alter their direction in a part of that course.

In the problems before the canoist will be found the combinations of every degree and variety of these rocks and currents, but the actual circumstances he has to deal with at any specified moment may—it is believed—be generally ranged under one or other of the six cases depicted in the accompanying woodcut.

In each of the figures in the diagram the current is

supposed to run towards the top of the page, and the general course of the canoe is supposed to be with the current. The particular direction of the current is indicated by the dotted lines. The rocks when shaded are supposed to be *sunk*, and when not shaded they are *breakers*.

Thus the current is uniform in figs. 1, 2, 3; and it is otherwise in figs. 4, 5, 6. The rocks are all sunk in figs. 1, 2, 3, and 5; whereas in figs. 4 and 6 there are breakers. The simplest case that can occur is when the canoe is merely floating without "way" through a current, and the current bears it near a rock. If this be a breaker, the current, being deflected, will generally carry the boat to one side. The steering in such cases is so easy, and its frequent occurrence gives so much practice, that no more need be said about it.

But if the rock be a sunk rock, and if it is not quite plain from the appearance of the water that there is depth enough over the rock to float the boat, then it is necessary to pass either above the rock, as in fig. 1, or below it, as in fig. 2. The black line in these figures, and in all the others, shows the proper course of the centre of the boat, and it is well to habituate oneself to make the course such as that this line shall never be nearer to the rock than one-half of the boat's length.

A few days' practice is not thrown away if the canoist seizes every opportunity of performing feats under easy circumstances which may at other times have to be done under necessity, and which would not then be so well done if attempted then for the first time.

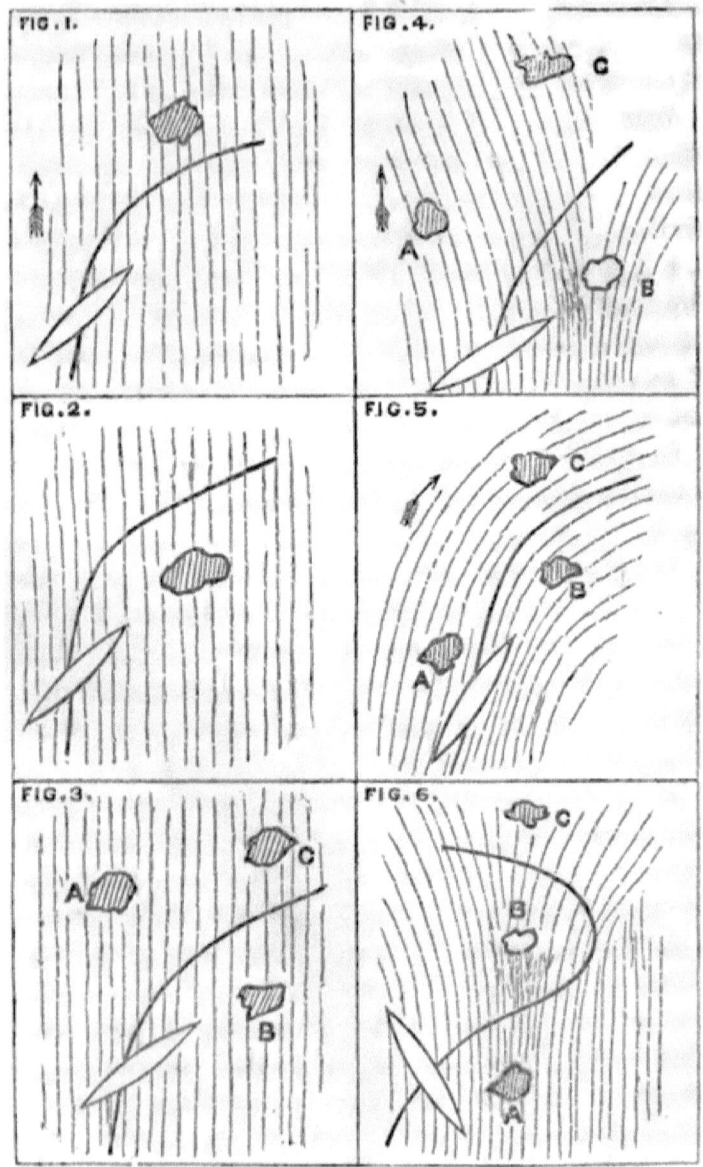

APPENDIX. 305

Let him, therefore, become adept in crossing above or below a single sunk rock with his *boat's bow pointed to any angle of the semicircle before him*.

Next we have to consider the cases in which more than one rock will have to be avoided. However great the number of the rocks may be, they can be divided into sets of three, and in each of the figures 3, 4, 5, 6 it is supposed that (for reasons which may be different in each case, but always sufficient) the canoe has to pass between rocks A and B, and then between B and C, but must not pass otherwise between A and C.

In fig. 3 the course is below B, and above C, being a combination of the instance in fig. 2 with that in fig. 1.

The precise angle to the line of the course which the boat's longer axis ought to have will depend upon what is to be done next after passing between B and C, and hence the importance of being able to effect the passages in fig. 1 and fig. 2 with the boat at any required angle.

We may next suppose that one of the three rocks, say B, is a breaker which will deflect the current (as indicated by the dotted stream lines) so as to modify the angle of the boat's axis, though the boat's centre, as in fig. 4, has to be kept in the same course as before.

It will be seen at once that if A were a breaker the angle would be influenced in another manner, and that if C were a breaker the angle at which the boat should emerge from the group of rocks would be influenced by the stream from *C* also; but it is only necessary to remind the reader that all the combinations and permutations of breakers and sunk rocks need not be separately discussed,—they may be met by the experience obtained in one case of each class of circumstances.

Fig. 5 represents a *circular current* in the group of three rocks. This is a very deceptive case, for it looks so easy that at first it is likely to be treated carelessly. If the boat were supposed to be a substance floating, but without weight, it would have its direction of motion instantly altered by that of the current. But the boat has weight, and as it has velocity (that of the current even if it is not urged also by the paddle so as to have "way" through the water), therefore it will have *momentum*, and the tendency will be to continue in a straight line, instead of a curve guided solely by the current. In all these cases, therefore, it will be found (sometimes inexplicably unless with these considerations) that the boat *insists* upon passing between *A* and *C*, where it must not be allowed to go, on the hypothesis we have started with; and where it effects a compromise by running upon *C*, this is by no means satisfactory.

This class of cases includes all those where the river makes a quick turn round a rock or a tongue *B*, where the boundary formed by the rock *A* and the outer bend of the stream is a solid bank, or a fringe of growing trees, or of faggots artificially built as a protection against the erosion of the water. This case occurs, therefore, very frequently in some fast rivers, say, at least, a hundred times in a day's work, and perhaps no test of a man's experience and capacity as a canoist is more decisive than his manner of steering round a fast, sharp bend.

The tendency in such cases is always to bring **the boat round by paddling forward with the outer hand,** thereby adding to the "way," and making the force of the current in its circular turn less powerful relatively. **Whereas, the** proper plan **is to back** with the **inner hand,** and so to stop all way in **the** direction of the **boat's** length, and to give the current its full force on the boat.

The case we have now remarked upon is made easier if either A or C is a breaker, but it is very much increased in difficulty if the rock B is a breaker or is a strong tongue of bank, and so deflects the current outward at this critical point.

The difficulty is often increased by the fact **that the water inside of the curve of** the stream may be **shoal, and so the paddle on** that side strikes **the** bottom **or grinds along it in backing.**

When the curve is all in deep water, and there is a pool after B, the boat ought not to be turned too quickly in endeavouring to avoid the rock C, else it will sometimes then enter the eddy below B, which runs up stream sometimes for fifty yards. Again, the absurd position you are thereby thrown into naturally causes you to struggle to resist or stem this current; but I have found, after repeated trials of every plan I could think of, that it is best to let the boat swing with the eddy so as to make an entire circuit, until the bow can come back towards B (and below it), when the nose of the boat may be thrust into the main stream, which then will now turn the boat round again to its proper course. Much time and labour may be spent uselessly in a wrong contest with an eddy.

In fig. 6, where the three rocks are in a **straight line**, and the middle one is a breaker, an instance is given when the proper course must be kept by *backing* during the first part of it.

We must suppose, then, that the canoist has attained the power of backing with perfect ease, and this is quite necessary if he intends to take his boat safely through several hundred combinations of sunk rocks and breakers. Presuming this, the case in fig. 6 will be easy enough, though a little reflection will show that it might be very difficult, or almost impossible, if it is in the power of the canoist to give only a forward motion to the boat.

To pass most artistically, then, through the group of rocks in fig. 6 the stern should be turned towards A, as shown in the diagram, and the passage across the current, between A and B, is to be effected solely by backing water (and chiefly in this case with the left hand) until the farthest point of the right of the curve is reached, with the **boat's** length still as before in the position represented in the figure. Then the forward action of both hands will take the canoe speedily through the passage between B and C.

Cases of this sort are rendered more difficult by the distance of C from the point above A, where you are situated when the decision has to be made (and in three instants of time) as to what must be done ; also, it would usually be imprudent to rise in the boat in such a place to survey the rock C from a nearer position.

If it is evident that the plan described above will not be applicable, because other and future circumstances require the boat's bow to emerge in the opposite direction (pointing to the right), then you must enter forwards, and must back between B and C, so as to be ready, after passing C, to drive forward, and to the right. It is plain that this is very much more difficult than the former plan, for your backing now has to be done against the full stream from the breaker B.

In all these cases the action of the wind has been entirely omitted from consideration, but it must not be forgotten that a strong breeze materially complicates the problem before the canoist. This is especially so when the wind is aft; when it is ahead you are not likely to forget its presence. A strong fair wind that has scarcely been felt with your back to it, and the swift stream and the boat's speed from paddling all in one direction, will suddenly become a new element in the case when you try to cross above a rock as in fig. 1, and find the wind carries you broadside on against all your calculations.

Nor have I any observations to make as to sailing among rocks in a current. The canoe would of course be directed solely by the paddle in a long rapid, and in the other places the course to be steered by a boat sailing would be the same as if it were being merely paddled, though the action of the wind has to be carefully taken into consideration when the manner of keeping to the course has to be devised. In all these things **boldness and skill** come only after a few lessons of experience, and the canoist will find himself ready and able, at the end of his voyage, to sail down a rapid which he would have approached timidly, with the paddle, at the beginning.

But perhaps enough has been said for the experienced oarsman, while surely more than enough has been said to show the tyro aspirant the varied work he has to do, and the boundless field of interesting circumstances which will occupy his attention on a **delightful river tour.**

The **following notes** are on miscellaneous **points :—**

(*a*) We are sometimes asked about such **a voyage as** this, "Is it not very dangerous?" There seems to me to be no necessary danger in the descent of a river in a canoe. If it is desired to make it as safe as possible you must get out at each difficult place and examine **the course, and** if the course is too difficult you may take the boat past the danger by land.

But if the excitement and novelty of finding out a course in the spur of the moment is to be enjoyed, then, **no** doubt, there is more danger to the boat.

As for danger to the canoist, it is supposed, *imprimis*, that he is well able to swim, not only in a bath when stripped, but when unexpectedly thrown

APPENDIX. 311

into the water with his clothes on, and that he *knows* he can rely on this capacity.

If this be so, the chief danger to him occurs when he meets a steamer on water (rare enough on such a tour); for if he is upset by it, and his head is broken by the paddle floats, the swimming powers are futile for safety.

The danger incurred by the boat is certainly both considerable and frequent, but nothing short of the persuasion that the boat would be smashed if a great exertion is not made would incite the canoist to those very exertions which are the charm of travelling, when spirit, strength, and skill are to be proved. Men have their various lines of exercise as they have of duty. The huntsman may not understand the pleasures of a rapid, nor the boatman care for the delights of a "bullfinch." Certainly, however, the waterman can say that a good horse may carry a bad rider well, but that the best boat will not take a bad boatman through a mile of broken water. In each case there is, perhaps, a little of *populus me sibilat*, and it may be made up for by a good deal of *at mihi plaudo*.

(*b*) It has been said that the constant use of a canoe paddle must contract the chest, but this is certainly a mistake. If, indeed, you merely dabble each blade of the paddle in the water without taking the full length of the stroke the shoulders are not thrown back, and the effect will be injurious; but exactly the same is true if you scull or row with a short jerky stroke.

In a proper use of the paddle the arms ought to be

in turn fully extended, and then brought well back, so that the hand touches the side, and the chest is then well plied in both directions.

In using the single-bladed paddle, of which I have had experience in Canada and New Brunswick with the Indians in bark canoes and log canoes, there seems to be a less beneficial action on the pectoral muscles, but after three months' use of the double paddle I found the arms much strengthened, while clothes that fitted before were all too narrow round the breast when put on after this exercise.

(*c*) In shallow water the paddle should be clasped lightly, so that if it strikes the bottom or a rock the hand will yield and not the blade be broken.

Great caution should be used in placing the blade in advance when it is meant to meet a rock, or even a gravel bank, otherwise it gets jammed in the rock or gravel, or the boat overrides it.

It is better in such a case to retard the speed by dragging the paddle (tenderly), and always with its flat side downwards, so that the edge does not get nipped.

(*d*) M. Farcôt, a French engineer, has lately exhibited on the Thames a boat which is rowed by the oarsman sitting with his face to the bow, and thus securing one of the advantages of the canoe—that of seeing where you are going.

To effect this, a short prop or mast about three feet high is fixed in the boat, and the two sculls are joined to this by their handles, while their weight is partly sustained by a strong spiral spring acting near the

APPENDIX. 313

joint, and in such a manner as to keep the blade of the scull a few inches from the surface of the water when it is not pressed down purposely.

The sculler then sits with his face towards the mast and the bow, and he holds in each hand a rod jointed to the loom of the corresponding scull. By this means each scull is moved on the mast as a fulcrum with the power applied between it and the water. The operation of feathering is partially performed, and to facilitate this there is an ingeniously contrived guide.

This invention appears to be new, but it is evident that the plan retains many of the disadvantages of common sculls, and it leaves the double paddle quite alone as a simple means for propelling a canoe in narrow or tortuous channels, or where it has to meet waves, weeds, rocks, or trees.

However, the muscular power of the arms can be applied with good effect in this manner, and I found it not very difficult to learn the use of this new rowing apparatus, which is undoubtedly very ingenious, and deserves a full trial before a verdict is pronounced.

(*e*) In a difficult place where the boat is evidently going too near a rock, the disposition of the canoist is to change the direction by a *forward* stroke on one side, but this adds to the force with which a collision may be invested. It is often better to *back* a stroke on the other side, and thus to lessen this force ; and this is nearly always possible to be done even when the boat appears to be simply drifting on the stream. In fact, as a maxim, there is always steerage way sufficient to enable the paddle to be used exactly as a rudder.

Y

(*f*) When there is a brilliant glare of the sun, and it is low, and directly in front, and it is impossible to bear its reflection on the water, a good plan is to direct the bow to some point you are to steer for, and then observe the reflection of the sun on the cedar deck of the boat. Having done this you may lower the peak **of your hat so as to cut off the direct rays of the sun, and its reflected rays on the water, while you steer** simply by the light on the deck.

(*g*) When a great current moves across a river to a point where it seems very unlikely to have an exit, you may be certain that some unusual conformation of the banks or of the river bed will be found there, and **caution should be used** in approaching the place.

This, however, is less necessary when the river is **deep. Cross currents of** this sort are frequent on the Rhine, but they result merely from unevenness in the bottom far below.

(*h*) The ripple and bubbles among weeds are so totally different from those on free water that their appearance **at a** distance as a criterion of the depth, current, and direction of the channel must be learned separately. In general, where weeds are under water, and can sway or wave about, there will be water enough to pass. Backing up stream against long weeds is so troublesome, **and** so sure to sway the stern round athwart stream, **that** it is best to force the boat forward instead, even if you have **to** get out and pull her through.

(*i*) Paddling through rushes, or flags, or other plants above the water, so as to cut **of a** corner, is a mistake.

APPENDIX. 315

Much more "way" is lost by the friction than might **be supposed.**

(*j*) The hard exercise of canoe paddling, the open-air motion, constant working of the muscles about the stomach, and free perspiration result in good appetite and pleasant sleepiness at night. But at the end of the voyage the change of diet and cessation of exercise will be **apt to** cause derangement in **the whole system, and** especially in the digestion, if the **high condition or** "training" be not **cautiously lowered into the humdrum** "constitutionals" **of more ordinary life.** Still I have found it very **agreeable to take a** paddle in the Rob **Roy up to Hammersmith and** back even in **December.**

(*k*) **Other pleasant voyages** may be suggested for the holiday of the canoist. One of these might begin with the Thames, and then down the Severn, along **the** north coast of Devon, and so by the river Dart **to Plymouth.** Another **on** the Solent, **and round the Isle of Wight.** The Dee might be descended by the canoe, **and then to the left through the Menai Straits.** Or a **longer trip may be made from Edinburgh** by the Forth, and into **the** Clyde, **and through the** Kyles of Bute to Oban; then along the **Caledonian** Canal, until the voyager **can** get **into the Tay for a** swift run eastward.

But why not begin at Gothenburg and pass through **the pretty lakes of Sweden** to Stockholm, and **then skirt the** archipelago **of** green isles **in the Gulf of** Bothnia, until you get **to** Petersburg?

For one or other of such tours a fishing-rod and an

air rifle, and for all of them a little dog, would be a great addition to the outfit.

In some breezy lake of these perhaps, or some rushing river, the little Rob Roy may hope to meet the reader's canoe; and when the sun is setting, and the waters sparkle sleepily, the pleasures of the paddle will be known far better than they have been told by the pen.

www.ingramcontent.com/pod-product-compliance
Lightning Source LLC
Chambersburg PA
CBHW021205230426
43667CB00006B/558